COUPLES CONNECT

Enrich Your

Love

Life

STERLING HOUSE PUBLISHING

By Bonnie Bair

Names: Bair, Bonnie | Author and Editor

Title: COUPLES CONNECT | by Bonnie Bair

Subtitle: ENRICH YOUR LOVE LIFE

Description: 1st Edition. | Peoria; Illinois: Sterling House Publishing, 2024

Subject: Communication and Relationships

Identifiers: LCCN 2024907631 print |

ISBN 979-8-9854171-4-2 paperback

Dedicated to My Husband, Todd

Chapter 1   Tools for Connecting

Chapter 2   Healthy Exchanges

Chapter 3   Intimate Connections

Chapter 4 Conquering Challenges

Chapter 5   Building Unity

Chapter 6   Creating Peace

Chapter 7 Nurturing Connections

Special Thanks To:

-My husband, for his sacrifice, love, and faithfulness for over 30 years.

-My daughter and her family, for challenging me and motivating me to grow and learn.

-My parents, for their sacrifices, love, and commitment to each other for over 65 years.

-My sister, for her years of guidance and encouragement.

-My clients, for sharing their experiences with me.

-Other family, friends, boyfriends, teachers, pastors, health professionals, students, neighbors, and strangers; for teaching me about life and relationships.

-My readers ☺

Foreword

COUPLES CONNECT is full of over thirty years of techniques/practices for creating intimacy and peace in relationships.

The information within COUPLES CONNECT is seldom repeated. It's a bit like a reference book. Refer to it often as you make adjustments and improvements in your relationship. The table of contents will be helpful in locating specific information. Feel free to use a notebook to write down ideas as they come to you. While not necessary, you may order the workbook that goes along with COUPLES CONNECT, to assist with learning and remembering. Both contain the "Relationship Map" and communication guides for use in communicating and connecting.

The goal is for you to enjoy more satisfying relationships with those you love. Applying the techniques, within COUPLES CONNECT, will help you achieve the intimate connections you desire.

Introduction

Relationships are the key to our existence. The better they are, the better we feel. Connecting as a couple depends on several things. A person's habits, thought patterns, health, emotions, communication practices, beliefs, the past, and current situations, can all affect how we connect with another.

From a seven year-long dysfunctional relationship, to a following thirty-two years of a healthy marriage and twelve years of working with couples, I have discovered techniques and strategies that work for mending and enriching love relationships, of which I am happy to share with you.

Please note, while it may seem backwards, the chapters in COUPLES CONNECT are presented in a specific order to bring healing as quickly as possible to most relationships.

Enjoy Connecting!

Chapter 1

Tools for Connecting

Let's begin. Two extremely effective tools for connecting are: *Affirmations* and the *Relationship Map for Happiness.*

Affirmations are one of the quickest ways to improve behavior and establish new habits for healthy and happier relationships.

I learned about affirmations from Brian Tracy. Affirmations are statements that are spoken out loud that proclaim and help us reach desired behaviors or goals.

Affirmations stated in the present tense, such as "We listen" rather than "We <u>will</u> listen," makes for faster goal attainment because "will" implies a future date that delays immediate progress.

Also, the more affirmations are repeated, the quicker behavior change or goal achievement occurs. When affirmations are proclaimed daily, a person can notice improvement within a couple of weeks.

Here are some affirmations for connecting.

"We think the best of each other."

"That was then. This is now!"

"We accept each other's limits."

"We accept responsibility for our own beliefs, attitudes, and behaviors."

"We keep our word to each other and do what we say we will do."

"We ask each other about their needs, concerns, and ideas."

"We listen to understand and think before responding."

"We acknowledge the feelings of each other."

"We state what we feel and need with ease."

"We speak the truth with love and acceptance."

"We value each other's unique abilities and viewpoints.

"We are thankful for each other and for what we have."

"We work together as a team."

The **Relationship Map for Happiness** is the other tool that is extremely effective in bridging great divides between people.

Relationships are most often similar to putting a 1000-piece puzzle together without seeing the puzzle box. Each person has an image of the perfect or desired relationship in their head. Often, the image is not communicated adequately to the other person. Imagine putting a 1000-piece puzzle together, without seeing the box. It can be done. However, it would take much longer and may be very frustrating.

My **Relationship Map for Happiness** is like a Material Safety Data Sheet or like the puzzle box to a 1000-piece puzzle. It gives you all the necessary information on the other person, so you can interact with them in ways that are helpful rather than hurtful.

When it comes to healthy and happy relationships, it's important to first know about love languages and their significance. Gary Chapman is credited with developing the concept of the 5 Love Languages; including Words of Affirmation, Physical Touch, Acts of Service, Quality Time, and Gifts. His premise is that we tend to love others in the ways we like to be loved, if it is not the way the other person prefers to be loved, they won't feel the love to the degree that we are trying to express it.

Speaking another's love language reduces fighting and solidifies the relationship. It makes it stronger. It also helps with healing. We have learned to treat others the way we want to be treated. Therefore, we most generally try to love others in the way we deem important. But if it's not the way the other person deems as important, we miss the mark.

When we learn to love others the way they truly value and need, then we truly love them. Love is a choice. As we choose to love others in the way they can understand and connect with us, it is then that we are truly doing unto others as we would have them do unto us. Who doesn't want to be loved in a meaningful way?

My **Relationship Map for Happiness** is designed to help identify what kinds of verbal, physical, service, time, and gifts, are important in the daily lives of those you love. It is derived from Gary Chapman's concept of the five love languages. I have added my own discovery of words of acknowledgment, words of connection, and the use of endearing terminology to Gary Chapmans' "words of affirmation" work. I have also included the frequency of such desired behaviors.

The **Relationship Map for Happiness** can be modified for any relationship – minus the section on intimacy. A modified copy of it can be found for parent-child relationships, siblings, or friends in my book called, <u>We Smile.</u> A relationship map for co-workers and roommates can be found in my co-authored book with Teresa McNeeley called, <u>Couples, Co-workers and College Roommate Relationship Maps: For Living and Working Peacefully Together</u>. Both are on Amazon and can be found by searching "books by Bonnie Bair."

Although the following **Relationship Map for Happiness** tool assesses day-to-day living preferences, it is fun to take the Love Language Evaluations created by Gary Chapman. They can be found in his books: <u>The 5 Love Languages for Couples</u> and <u>5 Love Languages for Children</u>.

The following **Relationship Map for Happiness** is created to guide any two people in identifying values, priorities, needs, and preferences for themselves. They can then give it to the other person to communicate their preferences. You may want to log these preferences in your phone for easy reference for using and sharing, when needed.

Relationship Map for Happiness

Words I Value Most *(Circle preferences/frequency)*

Words of Acknowledgement:
i.e. ***"You worked hard on _____."***

Desired: Daily, Weekly, Monthly, Holidays (verbal /or written?) Other: _____

Words of Praise:
i.e. ***"You look amazing." "You smell good." "You're good at _____."***

Desired: Daily, Weekly, Monthly, Holidays (verbal /or written?) Other: _____

Words of Connection:
i.e. ***"I like when you _____." "I like how you _____." "I love you." "I want you to _____." "I want to do _____ with you."***

Desired: Daily, Weekly, Monthly, Holidays (verbal /or written?) Other: _____

Endearing Terms:
When you call me Sweetie, Honey, etc.

Desired: Daily, Weekly, Monthly, Holidays (verbal /or written) Other: _____

Types of Touch I Value Most

Kisses, Hugs, Sitting Close, Holding Hands (Daily, Bi-Weekly, Weekly, Monthly)

Back Rubs, Foot Rubs, Touching on the Knee, Shoulder, Etc. (Daily, Bi-Weekly, Weekly, Monthly)

Types of Acts of Service I Value Most

Keeping Things Picked Up, Dishes, Trash (Daily, Bi-Weekly, Weekly, Bi-Monthly, Monthly)

Laundry, Clean Bathroom, Vacuum, Dust (Daily, Bi-Weekly, Weekly, Bi-Monthly, Monthly)

Lawn Care, Vehicle Care, House Projects (Bi-Weekly, Weekly, Bi-Monthly, Monthly)

Appointment Scheduling, Date Planning (Weekly, Bi-Monthly, Monthly, Quarterly)

Types of Time Spent Together I Value Most

Talking, Praying, Dining, Coffee or Snacking (Daily, 2-3 times a week, Weekly)

Walking, Exercising, Resting, Watching TV (Daily, 2-3 times a week, Weekly)

Shopping, Traveling, Movie/Play, Dancing, Hunting/Fishing, Racing, Sporting Events (Weekly, Bi-Monthly, Monthly, Quarterly)

Types of Gifts I Value Most

Wrapped /or **Unwrapped?**

Expensive /or **Inexpensive**?

Hand-made /or **Store Bought**?

Food, Flowers, Jewelry, Clothes, Car Parts, Tools, Sporting Gear, Magazines, Candy (Daily, Weekly, Bi-Monthly, Monthly, Holidays)

Vehicle, Trip, Other: _____
(Quarterly, Holidays, Yearly, Spontaneously)

Relationship Map – Relationship Values

Another thing I discovered about relationships and love languages is that it's very important to apologize and thank others in ways they value. For example, My Husband values a simple I'm sorry. I value more words.

Two very sincere people may offend each other by the way they attempt to apologize. Sometimes when you explain to a person who values a simple "I'm sorry," they may think you are blaming them or making excuses for your behavior. It will not be viewed as sincere.

Likewise, when a person who values apologies with explanations, is simply told "I'm sorry," they may get ticked off. The first thought might be, "Do they even know what they are saying sorry to?" This can be exasperating and cause more hurt.

It's important to know what the other person values as a sincere apology. The apology may be taken more sincerely if you pair the apology with the primary or secondary love language of the person you are apologizing to. For example, my husband might prefer a simple I'm sorry with a gift, at the same time, since his main love language is gifts. For me, it would be best for him to hug me and say "I love you!" with an apology, since two of my main love languages are words and physical touch. Apologies/acceptance of apology preferences are also included the Relationship Map for Happiness.

What I Value

Apologies that include: *(Circle preference/s.)*

"I'm Sorry."   *"I shouldn't have _____."*

"I didn't mean to _____."

"I'm sorry you're hurting."

"How can I make it up to you?"

*"I was thinking _____ and I was feeling
_____."*

"In the future, I will _____." Other
_____

Some people like to prioritize their selections by numbering the preferences they circled, in the order, they prefer them.

Acknowledgment and acceptance of apologies are equally important as apologies.

Acknowledgment/Acceptance of Apologies that include:

___ *"I forgive you."*   ___ *"No Worries!"*

___ *"Thank You!"*   ___ *I believe you."*

___ *"I know you didn't mean to ..."*

Other _____

*People like what they like and usually don't deviate. Even if the other person does not do it the way you like, if you can identify that they are doing things the way they like. You can recognize they are trying to love you the best they know how to. This reduces fighting and increases levels of satisfaction.

Try to identify what you value with a "Thank you!"

<u>A "Thank you" that includes</u>: (Circle preference/s and prioritize.)

_____ *A smile*   _____ *A hug*

_____ *A kiss*   _____ *A Touch*

_____ *A gift*   _____ *An act of service*

_____ *A "Thank you! I appreciate it."*

Other _____

*It's also important to know what kind of greeting the people you love value. If the greeting you give them is not valued, it sets the stage for the following time together to spark discontentment and argument.

The **Kind of Greetings** I Value include:

_____ *A smile*　　_____ *A Hug*

_____ *A Kiss*　　_____ *"Hi!"*

_____ *"How are you?"*

_____ *"Hi Beautiful" (Handsome)*

Other:

_____

Keep in mind, the other person doesn't need to do everything the way we like all the time. The purpose of the "Relationship Map" is to make it clear to the other person what we like. If we are not clear, and they are not clear with us, the less likely we are to know what kind of things the other person needs/wants. Knowing this information allows both to interact in more satisfying ways. I have found that, most generally, husbands do try their best to please their wives whenever possible. It is just wives can be so hard for them to figure out and vice versa.

Another part of the Relationship Map for Happiness that is helpful for people in all relationships, is that of identifying what kind of relationships the other person values.

What I Value Most in Relationships:

(Check or prioritize)

___ Adventure

___ Appreciation

___ Communication

___ Financial Stability

___ Gentleness

___ Honesty

___ Humor

___ Independence

___ Physical Intimacy

___ Politeness

___ Practical Help

___ Spontaneity

___Togetherness

___ Understanding

Relationship Map – Support/Environmental Needs

*Knowing who or what kind of support system a person needs, will give further insight into each person. A support system may look like this:

(Examples)

Husband – He calms me, fixes things, spends time w/me and makes me laugh.

Dog – Is happy to see me and likes to cuddle.

Daughter – Challenges me and is fun to talk with.

Sister – She encourages me.

My Support System and why:

_____ - _____

_____ - _____

_____ - _____

_____ - _____

_____ - _____

_____ - _____

_____ - _____

Relationship Map – Daily Needs/Challenges

Daily needs and challenges are also important to identify.

Hours of Sleep I need each night or day:

_____ hours

I function best in these kinds of environments:
(Check preferences)

___ Quiet   ___ Noisy

___ Busy   ___ Organized

___ Dark   ___ Clean

___ Messy   ___ Relaxed

___ Musical   ___ Bright

Things I need when I wake up: (i.e. quiet, coffee)

_____

Things I need when I get home: (i.e. snack, shower)

_____

Relationship Map - Struggles/Dreams

Things I find to be difficult: (This will give the other person clues as to how to be helpful.)

Examples: housework, short-term memory, sleeping, standing all day, fixing dinner when tired

_____   _____

_____   _____

Things I do that I don't enjoy: (This will give clues on what to help the other person with/or give insight into the sacrifices they make and what to acknowledge/thank them for.)

_____   _____

_____   _____

Things I enjoy doing by myself/or with others.

_____   _____

_____   _____

Things I dream about doing:

_____   _____

_____   _____

What I want from life:

_____   _____

_____   _____

What I want to learn:

_____   _____

_____   _____

Places I want to go:

_____   _____

_____   _____

_____   _____

Relationship Map for Happiness – Communication Timing and Intimacy Needs

*This part is intended for couples and their need to connect through communication and physical intimacy. If the needs of both individuals are not met, on a give-and-take basis, the relationship will suffer. Love is a choice. Knowing what each other needs, is critical.

When best for me to discuss things: _(Circle)_

Time: Morning   Lunch Time

After Work   At Evening Meal   Bedtime

Day: Any Day   M-F   Weekend
Days off from work

Specifications: _____

Examples: I would appreciate knowing what you want to discuss ahead of time and arrange a time to discuss issues of importance.

It is ok to talk with me anytime about anything.

You can talk with me at designated times about anything without prior notice. I will say if I need time to think about something.

I would like for you to discuss heavier issues with me via writing to simplify and expedite.

The worst time/day for me to discuss things:

_____

The worst time/day for physical intimacy:

_____

The best for me to be intimate: (Circle preferences)

> **Time:**   Any Time   Morning   After Lunch
> After Work   Bed Time
>
> **Day:**   Any   Monday   Tuesday
> Wednesday   Thursday   Friday   Saturday
> Sunday
>
> Days I'm not working   Other: _____

The Way/s I Prefer to be Approached when the Other Person Wants to be Close or Intimate:

___Say you love me.   ___ Send me a "Love text."

___ Kiss my neck.   ___ Touch my back.

___ Grab my body.   ___ A passionate kiss.

___ Take my hand and give me that "look."

___ Ask me if I want to fool around.

___ Ask me to join you on the couch or in bed.

___ Ask me to do something with you.

___ Rub my back or shoulders.

___ Help me finish what I am doing.

___ Other _____

Relationship Map – Emotional Needs

*Unmet expectations can cause much hurt and conflict when unaware of what a person needs. When preferences are identified, couples can be better equipped in how they choose to respond to each other in these various situations.

It's like having an owner's manual for your car. Knowing what to do and how to operate safely is valuable to others, in many cases. It should decrease fighting and increase satisfaction when the information is followed.

*It will be helpful to add any specifics, from the Relationship Map to your phone for easy reference. Especially since we often pair ourselves with someone who is opposite and these responses may not come naturally.

These are Ways I Prefer Others to Respond When I Look or Sound:

Sad/Disappointed or Am Crying

___ *Hug me.*   ___ *Tell me, "It will be okay."*

___ *Stay close by me.*   ___ *Say you understand.*

___ *Tell me you love me.*   ___ *Don't touch me.*

___ *Hold my hand.*   ___ *Touch my shoulder.*

___ *Ask if there is something I need.*

___ *Ask if you can help me with something.*

___ *Tell me I will figure it out.*

___ *Tell me you don't blame me for being upset.*

___ *Tell me we can talk later.*

___ *Go away and give me some time.*

___ *Say nothing!*

Don't _____.

Anxious/Overwhelmed:

___ *Tell me it will be okay.*

___ *Ask if there is something you can do for me.*

___ *Get out of my way. Do something helpful.*

___ *Pray for or with me.*

___ *Tell me you understand.*

___ *Tell me you are here for me.*

___ *Remind me to do Kegels and breathe.*

___ *Hug me.* Other _____

Don't _____.

Crabby/Complaining/Frustrated:

___ Hug me.   ___ Tell me, "It will be okay."

___ *Stay close to me.*

___ *Tell me you understand.*

___ *Tell me you love me.*   ___ *Don't touch me.*

___ *Hold my hand.* ___ *Touch my shoulder.*

___ *Ask if there is something I need.*

___ *Ask if you can help me with something.*

___ *Tell me I will figure it out.*

___ *Tell me you don't blame me for being upset.*

___ *Tell me we can talk later.*

___ *Go away and give me some time.*

   (___ minutes)

___ *Say nothing!*

Don't _____

Angry:

___ *Tell me, "It will be okay."*

___ *Stay with me.*

___ Ask me if I'd like to talk.

___ Don't touch me.

___ Touch my shoulder.

___ Ask if there is something I need.

___ Ask if you can help me with something.

___ Tell me we can talk later.

___ Tell me you don't blame me for being upset.

___ Tell me I will figure it out.

___ Go away and give me some time.

　　　(___ minutes)

___ Say nothing!

Don't _____

Happy/Excited:

___ Say, "I'm glad you're having fun."

___ Hug me or hold my hand.

___ Celebrate with me.

___ Touch my shoulder or kiss me.

___ Tell me you love me.

The following and final section of The Relationship Map for Happiness includes a section on discovering what each person feels is most respectful or loving. These specifics for showing respect can be major points of contention when we don't understand the perspective of the other.

These Kinds of Things Show Me Love/Respect the Most (Check preference/s.)

_____ Calling me by an endearing name in <u>public</u>

_____ Calling me by <u>my name</u> in <u>public</u>

_____ Calling me by an endearing name in <u>private</u>

_____ Calling me by <u>my name</u> in <u>private</u>

_____ <u>Not</u> contradicting or correcting me in <u>public</u>

_____ <u>Not</u> contradicting or correcting me in <u>private</u>

_____ Making decisions for me

_____ <u>Not</u> making decisions for me

_____ Giving me 2 things to choose from

_____ Open the car door/doors for me

_____ Let me open my own doors

___ Give me directions; like where to park.

___ Don't tell me what to do; like where to park.

___ Listen by restating what I said in your own words.

___ Listen, by cooperating with what I said and doing it.

___ Ask how you can help, don't tell me what to do.

___ Wait until I am finished with something, rather than interrupting me.

___ Let me lead when doing something together.

___ Lead me when doing something together.

___ Ask questions when doing things together.

___ <u>Don't</u> ask questions, when doing things together.

___ Support my interests and decisions, by asking me about them.

___ Support my interests and decisions, by accepting them without questions.

___ Ask me what I <u>feel</u> about things.

___ Ask me what I <u>think</u> about things.

___ Ask me if "I'm sure" of something, if you think something is not right.

___ Don't ask me if "I'm sure" of something; instead state your concern directly.

___ Be gentle with my feelings

___ Be direct and state what you need.

___ State what you observe and ask what I need, if something seems amiss.

___ State what you observe and ask what my plans are, when something seems amiss.

___ Show interest in me, by planning dates and family activities I would enjoy.

___ Show interest in me, by planning dates and family activities we can all enjoy.

___ Ask me if I want to X, when, you want to X.

___ Tell me you want to do something, and then ask me if I will join you.

Relationship Map Warning: Over time people tend to revert back to old habits and ways of interacting, so it will be necessary to periodically review the Relationship Map for Happiness. Now that it is clear to both of you what the other needs, enjoy the peace and extra time you have to spice up life together by doing activities to help others, or by going on trips, etc. You will now be more of a blessing to each other and those around you!

Chapter 2

Healthy Exchanges

Healthy exchanges are essential for couples to connect. My most challenging couples have helped me develop some simple communication formulas and guides. These are especially helpful when communicating difficult issues and emotions; especially during times of stress. The formula strategies below are proven to be effective for couples in connecting and to keep from fighting. These can be used in virtually every situation. ***Taking time to memorize and practice them will be of great value.***

Simple Communication Strategies

1. Communication 1,2,3,4

This formula helps couples to keep from fighting unfairly. It is the following: (It may require several exchanges before having full closure.)

1. *I feel* _____.”
2. *“I like, or I don't like, when* _____.”
3. *“I need or want* _____.”
4. *“Would you be willing to* _____?”

That's it! Keep it simple.

Examples of this formula are as follows:

> *I feel* afraid. *I don't like when* you talk to your old boyfriend. *I need* reassurance. *Would you be willing to* stop talking to him and show me your phone to prove it?

> "*I feel* encouraged. *I like when* you touch my back when sitting on the couch watching TV. *I need* to feel your touches like that. *Would you be willing to* do that more often?"

If a person doesn't like talking about their feelings, they can use steps 2-4.

For example:

> "*I like or don't like when* you leave the toilet seat up. *Would you be willing* to put it down when you are finished."

If a person does not like stating what they need, use steps 1, 2, and 4. For example:

> "*I feel* tired. *I don't like* talking when it's late at night. *Would you be willing to* talk about this at breakfast?"

You don't have to use all 4 steps. Three may be all that is necessary, like:

"I feel guilty. I don't like frustrating you. I need to be better at communicating my needs w/you."

You can even say 2 things like:

"I feel crabby. I need to eat."

Basically, using any of these four prefaces when communicating will help with connection and understanding.

They can even stand on their own. Example:

"I'm feeling misunderstood".

OR

"I like when you help me pay the bills."

OR

"I need some alone time to think".

OR

"Would you be willing to finish the dishes?"

A simple direct statement using one of the above prefaces may be all that is needed. Again, memorizing and practicing *"I feel..., I need..., I like..., Would you be willing to..."* will save you much time and anguish. It cuts out the fighting and helps with connecting.

2. I'm Thinking You're Thinking...

Another simple formula I discovered, can be used for initiating conversation and gently addressing issues you think may be of concern. It's what I call the I'm Thinking, You're Thinking Strategy. Competitive Couples especially enjoy it and can make a game out of it by seeing who can correctly guess what the other is thinking and feeling. This formula also helps reduce unfair fighting. It works as follows:

"I'm thinking you're thinking _____.

Is that what you're thinking?"

Or

"I'm thinking you are feeling _____.

Is that how you are feeling?"

Or

" I'm thinking you need _____.

Is that what you need?"

This exposes any misconceptions each person may be having.

3. Weekend Communication

It wasn't long after my husband and I were married, that we started noticing problems on weekends. We would often get into fights because we failed to communicate our needs about how we wanted to spend our weekend time off from work. One or both of us would get upset because of unmet expectations. After I realized what was going on, I made a little communication form to help us communicate with each other better. It was very effective, once we got used to using it, and the fighting over weekend stuff ceased. It went like this:

"What would you like to do today?

I'd like to _____ with you today."

When problems occur, remember these phrases to get past the unfair fighting:

"I'm sorry. Will you forgive me for _____?"

"I forgive you for _____."

Forgive yourself/move forward with the thoughts: "I forgive myself." "That was then. This is now."

Communication Help for Difficult Issues or When a Difficult History Exists

The following format will help communicate weighty issues between couples; especially when there has been previous fighting. It can be used during a scheduled talk time or during a date. It can help couples with connection and healing. (It is not necessary to complete every blank – only the ones that apply. Circle the words that apply, as well.) A feeling list follows.

"I have felt _____ for _____."

"I'm feeling _____because _____."

"I'm thinking you have been feeling _____

with _____ Because _____."

"I know you love me because _____."

"It really helped/bothered me when _____

_____because,

I have felt/needed _____

when this happens."

"I'm sorry. Will you please forgive me for

_____?"

"I'm willing to _____ and to

_____ in the future."

"From now on, I will do my best to _____

by _____."

"A way you could help me (if/when you see,

hear, or feel me _____, is to

_____.

It will help me to _____."

"I want/need you to understand _____.

I forgive you for _____."

"I want/need you to _____.

I understand you need me to _____

_____."

"Today I want to _____with/for you.

Would you be willing to _____?"

List of feelings:

abandoned, accepted, agitated, angry, annoyed, anxious, attractive, attacked, beautiful, betrayed, bored, conflicted, confused, curious, defensive, determined, devastated, disappointed, ecstatic, envious, exasperated, exhausted, frightened, frustrated, grieved, guilty, happy, helpless, hopeful, hurt, indifferent, innocent, interested, irritated, jealous, lonely, manly, mischievous, miserable, misunderstood, negative, optimistic, overwhelmed, paranoid, puzzled, regretful, relieved, sad, safe, satisfied, secure, shocked, speechless, surprised, stupid, suspicious, sympathetic, thoughtful, trapped, undecided, unsure, withdrawn, wonderful

Things to Remember when Dealing with Each Other in Difficult Discussions

- Think the best of each other.

- Acknowledge your part in the situation.

- Have an accepting attitude.

- Agree with each other as much as possible
    (You can agree to disagree.)

- Accept the other person as they are.

- Ask specific questions to make things clear.

- Ask for what you want and need.

- Ask how you can make things right/what you can do to make things better.

- Reward efforts, in the way each person likes.

- Remember: You are learning! The more you practice, the better you get at it.

- Remember: You are responsible for your own feelings, words, and actions.

- Instead of being offended, you can ask yourself; is there any validity in what they said?

It might help deal with feelings by thinking "what is the other person feeling and why would they say that?" This can help put things into proper perspective. Maybe they are hurt or not feeling well. Or they might just have a different perspective than us, or they present things differently. We can choose to think "It's ok." Regardless, when an insult occurs, it's like paying attention to a thermostat. Someone is not comfortable. We can choose to ask the other person how they are feeling and what they need. If we listen to them first, they will probably listen to us next. It is then that we can start negotiating a situation that is relatively comfortable for both of us. If we choose to get mad and respond badly, things may get worse.

When the other person says how they feel. It's important to name the feeling yourself, such as, *"Oh, you are feeling* _____." It may also help to comment on the feeling, such as, "I can understand how you would feel _____. Or "I want to understand, please tell more."

Communicating Suppressed Feelings

It is also sometimes easier to communicate via writing instead of verbally in the case when anxiety or defensiveness is an issue. I suggest couples who have tended to fight often or who typically don't communicate in healthy ways, to connect by communicating with a writing journal. The journal can be kept in a location that is convenient for both people. You can start by filling in the blanks below. •

"I feel _____ because _____.

"I like when you: _____."

"I like when we: _____."

Example:

"I feel sad because we don't talk much. I feel hesitant to tell you this because I don't want to hurt your feelings or be rejected."

"I have felt left out and unloved because you seem too busy for me."

"I like when you call me to ask how I am doing. I like when we do things together, like going out for coffee. I like being with you because you are special to me."

Further communication can be:

"When you see/feel/hear me _____

you can help by _____*."*

For example: When I seem crabby, you can help by asking me if there is something I need.

When Responding to Communication:

"I (understand/think) you've been feeling _____,

(because/when) _____*."*

"I understand you would like me to _____

*when*_____*."*

"I would like for you to _____

when you (see/hear/feel) me _____

because _____*."*

Following is an example:

> *"I understand you have been feeling left out. I think you are jealous of the time I spend with your sister. I understand you would like to have a closer relationship with me. I would like that too. When you are feeling left out, I would like for you to tell me. I'm sorry I have not spent time with you when you asked. Asking me ahead of time will help me arrange*

my schedule. I will make efforts for a closer
relationship in the future because you are
important to me, and I love you."

Communicating with a Quiet Person

Writing may also help a quiet person to express
more of what they are thinking or feeling.

Communicating with a quiet person can be
exhausting and frustrating. Silence can be used as
an unfair fighting and avoidance technique, which
has the potential to become abusive. Below are
some tips I have learned from various relationships
to keep conversations healthy when interacting
with a quiet person.

If you want to know what the person really thinks
and how they really feel, learn to ask them what
they think or how they feel about something prior
to you telling them what you think or how you feel.
(Otherwise, they might not want to disagree with
your thoughts, or they may feel like you are
imposing your thoughts or feelings on them.)
Note: *Often, they will say "I don't know," just before
they come up with an answer. Wait for the answer.
The "I don't know" is their first step towards a
response. They are thinking and processing.*

When you ask a question, try using the same type of wording they use when they ask you a question.

You might also consider giving them a heads up on what you'd like to discuss and ask when a good time is for them to discuss it. Individuals avoid communication usually because they need time to think about the same issue you have been thinking about for a long time. They usually don't want to be taken off guard and they may value accurate and less wording. They want to have well-thought-out responses.

You might ask them to write their thoughts and concerns out for you, so they can express more fully and you can respond better.

If they seem mad at you, you might ask them if they are mad at you and ask them what you said or did that hurt them. When you ask, ask in a way that says, *"I want to hear it and I'm sorry."* Be patient and wait! Offer that they can write it down - if it's easier for them to do so.

Assure them you will be patient and non-judgmental. Phrases like, *"It's ok,"* will help them communicate with you.

Tell them you need to know how they really feel because if you do not know, you cannot change your own behavior to ways that work better for them.

Tell them when you do not know how they feel, you don't feel connected, and you cannot satisfy them or make mutually satisfying decisions together.

Reassure them they are terrific, and you are grateful for them; even if they may say something that is hard for you to hear or say something you don't agree with. (Many times, the reason why the other person doesn't talk is, they don't want to make the other person feel bad or make the relationship worse.) Tell the other person it's harder on you when you don't know how they really feel.

After they do talk, be sure to be responsible for your own actions/behavior and thank them for sharing.

If it's your spouse, you might want to meet your spouse's need for physical contact, prior to talking. (It's easier for men to connect emotionally when there is physical contact. The physical connection helps men feel emotionally safer to share thoughts and feelings.) You might also explain to him that when he clams up (rarely talks, gives one-word answers, doesn't talk much, or give feedback on the things you say), you feel the same feelings as he might feel when/if you refused to be intimate.

Explain to them the more the topic is avoided, the greater anxiety you have and the greater and more frequent your need to talk about it becomes. Therefore, it will save both of you time and trouble to go ahead and discuss it.

Further, tell them they don't have to have all the answers. Guys typically feel pressure to know all the answers. When they don't know how to do something you ask or don't know how to address a problem, they can get crabby and avoid it.

Note: If you want the other person to talk more, try spending more time with them while being quiet. Wait patiently. See if they talk more.

When you ask a question and want more information, simply ask, "More details, please."

You can invite them to switch roles with you and interact how you interact with them. This should be an insightful exercise for both of you. The person that does not talk much, values quietness. They may see wordiness as annoying.

Say little and choose your words carefully. They may say more, and your relationship will probably become better connected and more enjoyable.

Thank the other person when they do talk to/with you! Be patient with each other as you make changes over time.

Communicating Feedback without Hurting Feelings

Healthy interactions and connections between couples require skills in giving feedback, without hurting feelings. I learned about the following technique from a friend who had learned it at a conference. You've probably have heard of it. It has three simple steps.

> **The Sandwich Technique** – *Build a sandwich.*
>
> 1. **Say something nice about the person.** (It's the bread.)
> 2. **Tell them what you need or like and why.** (It's the meat or sandwich filling.)
> 3. **Say something nice again and thank them for listening/caring.** (It's the bread.)

(Don't worry so much. They may appreciate your courage and honesty and love you more.)

Sandwich Example 1

1. *"I love you. You care about me".*
2. *"I like when you compliment me. It makes me feel valued by you".*
3. *"Thank you for listening to what I need, and thanks for loving me."*

Sandwich Example 2

1. *"You are important to me."*
2. *"I will enjoy our time together more when we can discuss more things I care about; Like asking me about how I am doing and what I enjoy and talking about some funny experiences you have had and sharing about things other than just politics or people."*
3. *"I hope you understand, and I look forward to getting together again soon, because I value you and our time together."*

Family Communications – Holidays

Family can be both a source of contention and or connection for couples. The above example of the Sandwich technique may need to be used prior to spending time with family for dinners and holidays if politics and gossip have been problematic.

I have found it helpful to **be prepared with discussion questions or stories to share when meeting with family members that haven't been seen in a while.**

Whenever possible, **it is also helpful to take care of any unfinished interpersonal issues in private, prior to attending family functions.**

Quick Communication Tips and Phrases

The following are quick communication tips and phrases that can assist in keeping healthy conversations and interactions for connecting.

For Women to Use with Men

"I love and respect you."

"Do you mind if _____?"

"Where and what's the plan?" "More details, please."

"I would like to help. What would be most helpful to you?"

"When is a good time for us to discuss _____?"

"What do you think I'm feeling?"

Would you be willing to _____?"

*Remember, the more direct you are, the easier it is for a man to respond. Think slow and steady. Be purposeful and say one thing at a time. Remember it helps them not to get overwhelmed and helps them to respond better.

For Men to Use with Women

"I love you."

"I understand what you are saying. You are saying
_____."

(This will save you from having to listen to things many times over. It will also help them feel how important they are to you.)

"It sounds like or seems you are feeling
_____." "Tell me more."

"Is there something you need me to do?"

"I don't blame you," or "I can see how that would be upsetting."

"I'm feeling overwhelmed."

"I know you will figure it out."

Remember, Women are feeling-oriented and need to know they have been listened to and their feelings are understood.

Chapter 3

Intimate Connections

Intimacy between a couple, includes both verbal and non-verbal communications for connecting.

A funny story about miscommunications comes from when my husband and I first started dating. One night after leaving the movie theater, Todd asked me, "What would you like to do now?" I was feeling a bit frisky and wanted to snuggle at his house. Although this was very clear in my mind, my verbal response was quite different. I said, "I want to go home. I'm tired." - meaning I wanted to go back to his house. Being the perfect gentleman he is, Todd promptly took me home and told me goodnight. When I tried to explain we could go to his house, he said, "You're tired, you should get some sleep." I felt disappointed, to say the least, and felt all rejected. I was especially upset when I could not reach him on the phone afterwards. He went somewhere without me, to boot! I thought he was breaking up with me. Thankfully this miscommunication saved me in my moment of weakness, as my goal was to wait until marriage. We have never regretted doing so. However, my husband's advice is: **"If you're frisky, just say so!**

Needless to say, I have learned to be more direct.

The following are some verbal communication phrases to enhance connections for intimacy.

Communication Phrases for Intimacy

"I like when you call me _____.*"*

"I like when you _____.*"*

"I like when I _____.*"*

"I like when we _____.*"*

"I like how you _____.*"*

"I like when you tell me I _____.*".*

"I like when you tell me you _____.*"*

"I love when you _____!*"*

"I want to _____.*"*

"I want you to _____.*"*

"I want you to know, I _____.*"*

"Do you want me to _____?*"*

Traffic Light Communication Method for Intimacy

A common frustration couples can have in relation to intimacy is determining when to pursue or not pursue the other. A couple I worked with gave me the idea of having a communication system based on a traffic light. Now, when she goes to bed she can put a green shirt, yellow sweater, or red scarf on the door. This communicates what kind of mood she is in for intimacy that night. The green shirt is the green light, if he is in the mood to proceed. He knows he should proceed with caution when there is a yellow sweater. He knows to respect her space when he sees the red scarf on the door. This solution is helpful in keeping hurt feelings at bay. Often times, men have told me that things would be much easier if they knew what kind of mood she was in. There are times in a relationship when roles (or needs) may be reversed, and it may be helpful for the other partner to communicate in this way.

Approaching Intimacy

The relationship map from chapter 1 has a section about identifying how the individuals within a couple's relationship, like to be approached when the other is in the mood to be intimate. I learned something from a female client when she used the analogy of getting into a pool as an explanation of the difference between her and her husband, in approaching intimate matters. It is brilliant! She explained her husband likes to dive right in, while she likes to dip her toes in first and take her time getting used to the water - before she gets in.

Pool Imagery for Intimacy

This information has helped me to assist other couples in better meeting their partner's intimacy needs. **Often, men tend to begin intimacy the same way. They often get into a pool by diving or jumping in.** Women tend to approach intimacy and the water more gingerly by getting their toes wet and getting used to the water much more slowly. If one person is not aware of what the other person likes, the approach to intimacy can either be frustrating or offensive. Imagine one person pushing the other person into the deep end of a pool – not always fun for both!

Since women's brains hook all things together, as opposed to men who can think about one subject at a time, it takes women a long time to process their feelings and get their head in the game, so to speak, prior to intimacy. This can be very frustrating for a man who is "ready" when a woman wants to talk about many things first. Because of this, it's important for a couple have a designated talk time out of the bedroom (earlier in the day or evening). It is best to have talk times when both individuals are functioning relatively well. When talk time is had daily, it leaves intimate time more sacred and enjoyable.

Communication via writing for Intimacy

Because each person is unique and has unique needs, **I encourage couples (especially those who have had issues in the bedroom) to have a discussion or write down specifics for each other. Specifics can include how they like to be approached, with the method and order preferred for things to be done, (including types of touches, kisses, phrases, etc.) with an approximate timing schedule.** *Men, especially take great pride in pleasing their women sexually. Knowing exactly what she likes can create great enjoyment and satisfaction for both, and give room for surprises along the way. Not knowing a key piece of information, might be a hindrance to exceptional lovemaking.*

An example of writing in specifics, is as follows: When I ask for a back massage, I like my back to be rubbed between my shoulder blades in a large circular motion, with medium pressure, and lasting a minimum of 30 seconds.

Using specifics, as in the back-massage example, makes it clear what is preferred. Therefore, each spouse can successfully meet the need or requests of the other. It takes the guesswork and "hit or miss" nature, out of it. *Please keep private information out of reach of children.*

Likes and Dislikes in Times of Intimacy

Don't be afraid to say when there is something you don't like. I have found if you include statements of what you do like, with something you don't like, it will be received better by the other person. An example of this is: "I really don't care much for when you _____, but I really like when you _____!"

Intimacy Logistics

Bedtime - *I suggest couples go to the same bed at relatively the same time every night together* (preferably around the time when the person needing to go to bed the earliest gets in bed); *even when not sleeping in the same bed through the night (for health reasons such as snoring or back issues, temperature differences, etc.). This allows for important snuggling and intimacy. In cases in which there is differing shift work or sleep schedules, etc.; that person can get out of bed and go take care of what they need to - after spending time together in bed.*

TV in the Bedroom

I also find it necessary to talk about TV. Since it is a huge distraction and can interfere with quality sleep (because of the blue light that awakes the brain) and can be the same as dumping garbage into your subconscious mind, if it is on during sleep (because your conscious mind isn't able to filter the information). *I recommend there to be <u>NO</u> TV in the bedroom, unless it is on only during certain times in which both individuals are awake.* In situations in which a person cannot fall asleep without noise, I recommend soft sounds or music w/out words. This allows the sub-conscious mind to rest, so you can function at your best.

Cell Phones

Remember to switch cell phones to *"Night Mode"* prior to bed. Blue light emissions tend to wake the brain and interfere with sleep. Keeping cell phone/facetime use limited to mutually designated times earlier in the evening will ensure marital harmony and quality sleep.

Children and Intimacy

I suggest that all couples have a designated date time and alternative date/time each week. This allows couples to prepare for intimacy without the worry of children. *Remember to lock the bedroom door when children may be around.*

Relationship Secrets

The following are some secrets I have discovered that will help couples connect and improve intimacy.

Secret 1

One person in a couple usually just wants a simple "I'm sorry." The other person usually wants an explanation with an apology.

When the person that likes explanations apologizes to the person that sees explanations as not accepting responsibility, it irritates and hurts the other person and comes across as insincere. It ends up doing the opposite of the intention.

When the person who doesn't like explanations just says, "I'm sorry," the person who likes explanations thinks they are just saying it to get the other person to shut up or that they are just saying it because the other person is upset.

The person they are apologizing to does not believe or think the other person fully understands or knows what was even so upsetting. They can get hurt and more frustrated. Therefore, the "I'm sorry" does not have the impact that the person saying it may have meant.

And it goes on and on.

It's helpful when both people recognize and discuss

71

what kind of apologies they value. Give the other person the kind of apology they value. It will save you tons of time and heartache in the future.

Secret 2

When a husband refuses to engage in conversation with his spouse, the rejection she feels is the same to her as the rejection he feels if she would refuse to make love physically with him.

Since conversation is foreplay for women. The satisfaction a husband feels when he physically satisfies his wife is like the desire and satisfaction she has for communication and meeting her man's emotional needs and vice versa.

It takes both people to move out of their comfort zone and choose to love the other in the way the other needs loved.

Secret 3

Women need to feel loved and cherished as worthwhile and "smart."

The secret is: in general, your man already values you as worthwhile and smart. Otherwise, he would not be with you. He just hasn't told you that. It often doesn't seem that way when you have seen their looks of confusion and shakes of the head. Truth is, they just do not understand. Admitting so might make them look not so smart. They have the need to be loved and cherished as worthwhile and smart individuals too.

Men: *Compliment the woman you love. Let her know you appreciate her. Tell her when you believe she has a good idea about something.*

Secret 4

Besides needing respect, men need to be admired physically.

The secrets are: Men need to be acknowledged not only for the way they provide for their spouse but also for how well they satisfy them. Sh... They need to have their intimate aspect admired.

Wives: *Be sure to compliment his body, as well as his ability to satisfy and provide for you.*

Secret 5

The spouse that doesn't talk much, values the spoken word and is quiet. They may view wordiness as annoying. Sh... They also often say "I don't know," before saying something, "Important." *Wait patiently.*

Try just being with the other person. Go where they are. Stay quiet and speak sparingly with choice wording. Be patient. Ask simple phrases like, "What do you think about _____? "Keep your thoughts to yourself, until later or until asked. When you would like to hear more from the other person when they say something, try a simple phrase like: *"More details, please?"*

The less you say, the more they may say, and the better your relationship may become.

Secret 6

"Would You Want To ..." has a different meaning to men than to women.

To Men: "Would you want to..." really means, "I really want to ... and I really want you to agree.

To Women: "Would you want to...?" simply means, "Do you have interested in....?"

Not knowing this, can cause a man to get upset and feel rejected by a woman when she does not realize how important the question is. I think this secret exists because men are more casual when they ask women to do certain things. They tend not to say when they really want to do something, unlike women that tend to say when they really want to do something. Likewise, if a woman asks a man if they want to do something a man might do it even though they really don't want to and then be unhappy about it; when it really didn't matter to the woman, because she was just wanting to know if he had an interest in it.

* This may not be a difference between men and women, but instead a difference in communication styles between someone who communicates more and someone who communicate less. However, I have seen commonalities in men and women within my counseling sessions with clients.

Secret 7

Women can feel lonelier when a man is at home and watching TV or playing video games than she does when he is not around.

The secret is: Women get offended when their man does not communicate with them. Men often do not realize this, since they are often happy and content to be around the woman they love, without talking. It is not the same for women.

Men: Talk to her when the commercial is on or ask what she would like to watch on TV. Do your best to watch something on TV you both will enjoy. Take turns watching each other's favorite show. Invite her to play a video game with you or take breaks from gaming to let her know you love and care about her and take time to ask about what she is doing.

Chapter 4

Conquering Challenges

Health Issues

The first challenge we will discuss is health issues. How we care for our bodies affects our lives and relationships. The quality of food or nutrients and medicine we take, sleep, and the exercise we get; all help determine the quality and length of life we spend with those we love. All of these elements can interfere with a couple connecting.

Health Issues that Affect Our Bodies/Relationships

1. Inadequate sleep

We all know how important sleep is to our bodies. According to the Koala Center for Sleep, inadequate sleep can lead to depression and anxiety. Sleep apnea and TMJ issues affect the quality of sleep. If you suspect either one, it's worth it to get treated. Seek out professional help as necessary. Many of my clients have benefited by taking 250 mg of magnesium, prior to bedtime since it can help relax the nerves. Others have noticed an improvement in sleep when they have taken 2.5-5 mg of chewable melatonin. Others benefit from taking both magnesium and melatonin together. There are other treatment options for poor sleep. If sleep is an issue, please discuss it with your doctor, as it affects your health/relationships.

Affirmations that can help with sleeping are:

To sleep better: ***"I sleep like a rock!"***

To stop the mind from racing when trying to sleep: ***"I stop thinking and start sleeping!"***

2. Inadequate Magnesium Intake

Not only can magnesium help with sleep, it can help also prevent depression, anxiety, migraine headaches, acid reflux, and muscle cramps. Often, clients report feeling happier and less anxious after a week of taking up to 250 mg/day of magnesium. Larger doses have the potential to affect the heart's rhythm, so contact medical professionals with any questions.

3. Inadequate Vitamin D Intake

Inadequate supplies of Vitamin D, especially in the winter months, can contribute to depression. I have suggested those with seasonal affective disorder (who are depressed in the winter months) take Vitamin D once the time changes in the fall until the time changes again in the spring. In the winter months, some of us do not get adequate doses of sunlight for our body to produce enough Vitamin D on its own. Not having enough vitamin

D can negatively affect the heart. Again, seek medical advice from a physician.

4. Inadequate Breakdown of Folic Acid

I learned from Dr. Matthew Preston, that some families do not carry the gene that adequately breaks down folic acid. L-methyl folate is a more elemental form of folic acid that can be used easily by the body. It may take the body weeks or months of supplementation with l-methyl folate to reverse depression or anxiety caused by inadequate utilization of folic acid.

5. Anxiety

Caffeine and artificial sweeteners can contribute to anxiety. Reducing intake of both should help reduce anxiety. ***Doing a Kegel exercise with any worry thoughts can help reduce anxiety significantly over time.*** According to a conference I attended by J. Eric Gentry, Ph.D., a <u>Kegel</u> exercise will help to reset the Vagus nerve (The main nerve that runs from our brain to our pelvis) and will send peaceful signals to the body; rather than stress signals. It causes the body to breathe deeper. It also helps the brain map new pathways for dealing with stress. The body cannot hold a peaceful and stressful response at the same time. It's one or the other.

Remember, anxiety is a signal to the body to do something. It usually requires you to do something; talk to someone, ask for help or take some other action. When something is totally out of our control; we can pray, do a Kegel, take a deep breath and let it go, or forget about it.

As stated earlier, inadequate processing of folic acid, low levels of magnesium, and inadequate sleep can all contribute to anxiety. Clients report less panic when they begin taking magnesium. Holy Basil can help with Social Anxiety. Do your research and ask your doctor.

6. Depression

Magnesium is often also helpful in treating depression. Clients generally report noticing improvement in mood after a week of supplementing with magnesium.

Some clients with anxiety and depression report a noticeable reduction of symptoms when they take St John's Wart. It's important to note that St. John's Wart should not be taken with any other anti-depressants, nor should it be taken by anyone with Bipolar 1 disorder.

There are various medical factors that can contribute to depression and irritability: inadequate sleep, low magnesium levels, low hormone levels, inadequate processing of folic acid, low levels of vitamin D, etc.

Moderate to severe depression is serious and needs attention. Consultation with medical professionals for testing and treatment options can make life much more manageable.

7. Diabetes/Hypoglycemia

Blood sugar issues can cause irritability and mood swings. Monitoring blood sugar levels is essential for stabilization and management.

8. Drug or Alcohol Usage

Substance use and abuse can contribute to mental health issues. Or, in many cases, individuals use drugs or alcohol to self-medicate an undiagnosed mental health condition such as anxiety, depression, bipolar disorder, etc. There is a medicine available to help people stop using drugs and drinking. One can ask a medical doctor or psychiatrist for help - if that is the case.

9. Gluten Intolerance

Individuals with gluten intolerance may have anxiety, depression, or bipolar-type symptoms. Genetic testing can be done to verify. However, a person, who is gluten sensitive, usually improves once they avoid gluten.

10. Bipolar Disorder

Anxiety and depression are present in bipolar disorder. *Medications having mood-stabilizing properties are essential for treating bipolar disorder.* Bipolar 1 disorder is different from Bipolar 2 disorder. *Regular anti-depressants, without any mood-stabilizing properties, can make bipolar disorder (especially bipolar 1 disorder)* **worse.** Also, Estrogen (or the birth control pill) can interfere with bipolar medication, making it less effective in treating bipolar disorder. A combination of over-the-counter lithium orotate (5-10 mg) or CBD, ashwagandha (400-800 mg nightly) and 1000 mg flaxseed oil can be helpful in managing bipolar disorder for a time. Both Lithium orotate and CBD can help reduce anger and stabilize mood. Ashwagandha helps elevate mood without causing mania. It also can help with stress and focus, thus helping with time management and punctuality. Cold pressed flaxseed oil can also help with mood stabilizing and depressive symptoms. While nutrients may not be a replacement for conventional medicine, they can certainly lessen the amount of medicine that is needed. Again, speak with doctors.

Please note: Only use Tylenol (Acetaminophen) for pain relief, when using over-the-counter lithium orotate or prescription lithium, to protect kidneys.

Also, anyone allergic to sweet potatoes should avoid ashwagandha.

Regardless of the issue, it is important to take responsibility, do your research and check with medical/mental health professionals to accurately pinpoint and treat these various medical issues.

Please note: Psychiatrists have four additional years of medical training directly related to the brain/medicines than general physicians do.

I'm including the following section on bipolar disorder because untreated bipolar disorder can cause havoc in any relationship. It is common for people with depression to gravitate towards people with bipolar 1 disorder and vice versa. The highs of bipolar disorder bring the person with depression up and the person with depression brings stability to the person with bipolar disorder.

Bipolar Disorder

Having bipolar disorder is not a sin or something to be ashamed of. According to the National Institute of Mental Health, "bipolar disorder affects approximately 7 million adult Americans, or about 2.8% of the U.S. population age 18 and older, every year. Bipolar disorder is usually always inherited. There is some research that shows head injury can cause bipolar disorder. It is often misunderstood, undiagnosed, and inadequately treated. Therefore, I'm taking the time to educate others regarding it.

First, what is bipolar disorder?

People with bipolar disorder tend to be very creative, compassionate, and intelligent. Individuals with bipolar disorder often have difficulty with distraction, racing thoughts, memory, anxiety, ADD or ADHD type symptoms, and have sudden changes in mood/behavior/sleep patterns/energy level. Early indicators of the disease can be crying easily and uncomfortable clothing or tags in shirts being problematic. High irritability or silliness can also be symptoms of such.

Some *individuals with bipolar disorder may have issues with the following:*

1. Drug or alcohol addiction: Persons with bipolar disorder often unknowingly self-medicate through alcohol or drugs. During a manic cycle (when things get overwhelming and out of control) they may subconsciously use alcohol or marijuana to level themselves off, so they can cope with things better. During a depressed cycle, they may use drugs or alcohol to help them not care about things so much. Without

medication, they desire drugs or alcohol for stabilization and survival.
2. Spending sprees or gambling problems
3. Suicidal thoughts or attempts (can indicate bipolar 2 disorder)

It is important to see a psychiatrist for accurate diagnoses and treatment if bipolar disorder is suspected, especially if another family member has bipolar disorder. Improper or inadequate treatment of bipolar disorder can be dangerous. I have found regular medical doctors do not always know how to treat bipolar disorder accurately. Sometimes they may treat it with a regular anti-depressant, which can make things worse. Accurate communication of the symptoms and asking questions about medications with mood-stabilizing properties will help regular physicians and psychiatrists to select the best medication for yourself or your loved one. Often it is necessary to try more than one medication or a different dosage of medication, to successfully manage bipolar symptoms.

Each person is different and may respond differently to medications. It's essential to communicate and follow up closely with the medical provider; especially when a person is not feeling well on a certain medication. Stopping the medication without medical supervision can make things worse and will not give the professional the opportunity to provide the individual with another medical solution. Bipolar disorder usually always requires medication or some nutrient to support the body. There is a chemical imbalance that needs to be addressed. Bipolar symptoms tend to get worse with age and stressful situations. It's important to have medication in a person's system, so they can handle stressors when they happen: like a computer needs a surge protector when it's lightening. There is some research regarding nutritional alternatives to medicine for treating bipolar disorder. Often, individuals with bipolar disorder are very against taking any medicine or may experience bothersome side effects from medication. However, it does need treatment in some way, for the person to function at their best for living and having happy relationships. It's important to do extensive research/or check with the professionals before treating bipolar disorder. The kind of treatment will depend on the type of bipolar disorder it is. Bipolar disorder often shows up during a person's early to mid-twenties.

How to Manage Bipolar Disorder

It is very important for individuals with bipolar disorder to get adequate regular sleep (7-10 hours per night) and eat healthy foods at regular intervals, as a lack of sleep and skipping meals can trigger manic episodes. A moderate exercise routine and daily quiet time are also essential for managing stress. Slowing down and keeping the number of activities and expectations to a minimum - especially during times of stress and taking daily nutrients/medication (until a cure is discovered) is imperative. Practicing routines with variety, prevents boredom. An example of this is to eat at the same approximate time each day and vary what you eat, where you eat, or who you eat with. Individuals with bipolar disorder tend to become bored, very easily. Planning ahead is helpful.

Individuals with bipolar disorder can often feel judged by others and feel more inadequate, overwhelmed, frustrated, and angry when others don't understand.

Family and friends of individuals with bipolar disorder might feel inadequate and scared because they don't know how to help or what to do. Remember, you can simply let the person know you care and ask them how you can help. Being willing to do something for them in exchange for them getting help and taking their medicine and nutrients can be helpful. It is also often helpful for someone to accompany them to doctor appointments for complete information sharing with health providers for adequate medical management. Education and an atmosphere of understanding, and acceptance will be helpful.

Our Spirit

Our Spirit plays a role in affecting our mind, body, emotions, and relationships. Just as we need adequate food, sleep, and exercise to maintain our bodies, we also need to tend to our spiritual needs. Practicing these seven spiritual practices will positively affect our relationships/lives.

1. **Being thankful helps our relationships with God and others and causes us peace.**

    Let the peace of God rule in your hearts, to which you were called in one body, and become thankful. **Colossians 3:15**

2. **Listening helps us gain understanding, builds relationships, and causes happiness.**

    Everyone must be quick to hear, slow to speak, and slow to anger. **James 1:19**
    Happy is the person who finds wisdom and gains understanding. **Proverbs 3:13**

3. Giving to others helps not only others but also helps ourselves.

   Give and it shall be given unto you. **Luke 6:38**

4. Going to God when we need something helps us and our relationships. God wants to help us with our everyday life issues and concerns.

   In every situation, by prayer and petition, with thanksgiving, present your requests to God. And the peace of God will be with you. **Philippians 4:6-7**

5. Seeking God daily, helps us to love others and be blessed ourselves. Reading God's word helps us to hear and follow accurately.

   Blessed is the person who listens to me (God), watching daily at my doors, waiting at my door-way. For those who find me, find life. Those who fail to find me, harm themselves. **Proverbs 8:34-36.**

   A day that begins and ends in prayer won't become unraveled. **Psalm 92:1-2**

6.   Making sure we have a day to rest each week allows rejuvenation in our body and spirit. It helps us to be at our best for others.

   Remember the Sabbath Day to keep it holy. Six days you should labor and do all your work; but the seventh day, is the Sabbath of the Lord (**Exodus 20:8**), and you should rest.

7.   Listening to God's word builds our faith for healing and miracles. God wants to do the impossible in our lives.

   Faith comes by hearing the word of God.
   Romans 10:17

   Faith is the substance of things hoped for, the evidence of things not seen. **Hebrews 11:1**

Differences - Biological

The second set of challenges to conquer for couples to connect at optimal levels, are the biological and social differences between men and women.

Physical Connections is to Men as Emotional Connection is to Women

I think I first heard from Gary Smalley that women connect emotionally, and men connect physically. Usually, men need a physical connection to feel safe and want to connect emotionally. Women need an emotional connection to want to connect physically. It takes both people to move out of their comfort zones and choose to love the other person in the way the other needs to be loved. Taking turns is a wonderful solution.

Men are at a disadvantage in winning arguments with women.

According to Gary Smalley, ***Men use only one side of their brain in communication, while women use both sides of their brains.*** This makes women's stories and emotions hard to follow. Because of this, women often misunderstand and think men don't care. This contributes to hostility from women and avoidance by men.

It typically takes a man longer to process and respond appropriately, due to having 6.5 times more "gray matter" (thinking matter) in the brain. Women have 9.5 times more "white matter" in the brain. It connects parts of the brain together and allows women to respond and communicate more quickly. ***Therefore, it helps if women are more direct with communication and give men time to respond to one thing before bringing up another item.***

It's important to know how men's and women's brains are designed, for stronger connections.

Women have fewer red blood cells and therefore, tire more easily. They are more emotionally responsive and therefore, laugh and cry more easily. Women are more verbal and relational than men and tend to be kinder and more people oriented. Therefore, they will care about who is involved and will enjoy solving problems together more than men will. Women are usually better at multi-tasking and are global thinkers. This can cause them to be more prone to becoming over-whelmed. Women revisit emotional memories and analyze them. They are faster and more accurate at identifying emotions. Because women feel closer and more validated through talking, they can get frustrated easily when their male counterpart is not as communicative with them.

On the other hand, men have more blood and muscles than women, which makes men typically stronger than their women counterparts. They are less sensitive to the cold and have larger brains and thicker skulls. They think about and seek sex more than women do. Sex is how men express their softer side. Men tend to be more focused and have better follow-through because of it. They often keep problems to themselves and like to solve problems alone. Men tend to be linear thinkers and can separate themselves from problems. They reflect more briefly on emotions and because of it, may frustrate their female counterparts when they don't want to discuss things at length.

Men and women approach problems with similar goals, but with different considerations. Problems arise when we expect the opposite sex to think, feel, or act the way we do. As we understand and accept our differences, we will be less frustrated with each other. We will compromise and get along better.

There are some exceptions to the above male/female differences. In some cases, certain things may be reversed in some couples. Usually, the main differences exist in every couple, due to opposites attracting. This awareness is helpful.

The above sources, for the information on the biological differences between Men and Women, are: Gary Smalley, Michael Conner, Web M.D., Psychology Today, Lawrence Wilson, MD, Athena Health, and Dr. James Dobson.

Differences – Social

Over the years of working with couples, *I have found that men often feel it is their job to please their spouses. Because of this, they tend to avoid sharing things that might be upsetting;*

especially those things that make their spouse cry. Their lack of sharing can be offensive to the women they live with. Then they can feel more inadequate when their spouse is more upset. They are known to say things like: "Don't worry about it!" This minimizing of concerns their spouse has can come across to their spouse as if they don't care, which is usually quite the opposite of what is happening. It's because men **do** care and don't want their wives to be upset.

Similarly, women have been socialized to please the men in their lives. Because of this, they tend to give beyond what they are comfortable. In doing this, resentment can build. They can become very unhappy and occasionally unwilling to continue with the relationship.

Men are programmed that it's their job to provide for their spouse and to fix things. This often can result in men putting their needs aside for so long that it builds resentment and then they are more irritable and difficult to live with. Or it can result in men trying to fix a problem without acknowledging their wife's feelings to their wife. *Since feelings are so important to women, it's important their husband acknowledges and understand their feelings.*

Conversely, women can make men uncomfortable when talking about feelings. As we learned earlier, men are not as good at identifying feelings or communicating. The difference is magnified because historically, girls practice talking about and identifying feelings; while boys are often taught to shake things off- so to speak. It makes the contrast between men and women greater and can make getting along more difficult.

Beliefs that Cause Problems

Beliefs that affect our relationships in negative ways is a third challenge to overcome. As relationships can be affected by differences, couples can also get stuck and fail to connect when they don't share what they think, how they feel, or if they don't respect or listen to each other fully.

Awareness is the key.

The following are some common beliefs that block communication, respect, and listening. They come from a conference by **David Burns, MD**. I have listed the most common beliefs from his work below that I've also observed when working with couples. Reviewing them will help identify stumbling blocks in your own communication.

Beliefs that block sharing of thoughts/needs:

- It's too painful to admit I'm part of the problem.

- I can't say how I feel because you are upset.

- I will punish you with silence and maintain my innocence.

- You should know what I want/feel without me saying.

- Conflict is dangerous.

- I must always please others or I shouldn't get angry.

- I've tried everything, but nothing works.

Beliefs that block listening/respect;

- I'm right. You are wrong. This is <u>your</u> fault. Or I don't want to be respectful.

- I must argue and defend myself.

- They will never change.

- I'm not causing the problem. I'm the victim and I have the right to get even.
- I'm entitled to better treatment or I'm too angry.

- One of us must win and one of us must lose. Or, it won't do any good.

- I don't want to get hurt again. Or why should I treat them well?

- I will keep you at a distance.

- You should think, feel, and behave the way I expect.

Affirmations for Healthy Interactions

The following affirmations will help with connection and interacting fairly with each other.

"I take responsibility for my own feelings, attitudes, and behaviors."

"I think the best of others and treat them with the respect I would want to be treated with."

"If someone does or says something I don't like, I can ask them to simply tell me why they are upset. I then can ask for what they need."

"I acknowledge and discuss concerns with the other. If I need time to think before responding, I ask for time to gather my thoughts to present/address concerns as needed (and in writing, if necessary)."

Emotions

Emotions also play a big part in whether a couple connects or not. Negative emotions can amplify problems and cause disconnection. Learning how to manage them is important for connecting with each other.

Frustration is commonly experienced before feeling anger.

Frustration is felt when there are misunderstandings with others or when you are unable to do the things you want to do or use to do. It also happens when there are unmet expectations or needs – leading to disappointment and sometimes anger.

Minimizing frustrations as best as you can, will help keep anger away. Having realistic expectations of yourself and others will help too. Things such as repeated scheduling difficulties and miscommunications (due to not having enough time, etc.) can be decreased by better time management, or simply doing fewer activities. Taking time to rest and making time for God and his word can help prioritize one's life and lessen frustrations.

They say **anger** is a secondary emotion that follows other negative emotions such as grief, worry, embarrassment, guilt, and fear.

Anger is a warning indicator light like your engine light on your vehicle. It requires immediate acknowledgment and attention. It's like an alarm. If you ignore it, bad things can happen. For example, if you ignore your alarm clock, you might be late for work and get fired. If you ignore a fire alarm, you may get burned. (In rare instances it may be important to ignore if the anger response has become a habit or gets worse with attention).

Alarms are created and set for a reason. Anger is our/others' alarm system.

The alarm of anger signifies there is immediate danger of a perceived or real threat to a system, either internal or external. Anger is valid and requires acknowledgment and attention.

Unexplained or frequent uncontrolled anger usually signifies:

    A. *When something is going on within the system (the person) itself.*

        - More than likely, nutrients are depleted and the body is not functioning as it's designed. It is malfunctioning and is especially sensitive to certain triggers and is more susceptible to stress.

- As nutrients are replenished, the person will heal.

B. ***When anger happens with a particular trigger*** - This signifies an *adjustment in perception or communication* is needed.

Ask yourself:

1. Is the anger due to the *continual ignoring* of concerns within your*self* or the expressed concerns of *others*?

2. Is the anger due to: Not asking?   Not telling?   Not   caring?   Not apologizing?

3. Or does the anger happen because of being too busy or having too many distractions and interruptions?

4. Does the anger stem from a lack of preparation?

5. How much of the anger is from frustration from someone perceiving you as bad or yourself perceiving someone else or yourself as bad.

6. Or is the anger from misunderstandings – of what you or someone else said, meant, or did?

How to Manage Your Anger

1. Stop/Assess the cause(s) of anger

2. Make sure internal systems are working properly.

3. Replenish or store up supplies
   - Consider nutrients (such as omega 3's, vitamins, eating different foods, herbs that help with stress or mood-stabilizing medication.
   - Do your research!
   - Ask an expert

4. Take care of your body!
5. Practice Relaxation – Breathing & Kegels

6. Practice Purposeful Thinking.
7. Prepare for/or avoid triggers.
8. Follow the plan.

If something happens unexpectedly and requires emergent action – Ask for help!

If there is a difference in opinion between you and someone else, stop and think. Do not do something you are not okay with or that you are

unwilling to do! You have permission to say "No."
There is a reason for the unwillingness. Ask the
other person to address your concern, before
agreeing or proceeding. Be willing to address the
other person/s concerns, as well.

When anger happens in response to *frequent*
stimuli, that happens at *expected and*
unexpected times.

> Prepare ahead of time.
>
> > 1. Your thinking
> > 2. Your response strategy
>
> Examples: If you prepare for others to be
> clueless or inconsiderate, you will not get as
> upset.
>
> If you prepare for losing track of your keys
> or phone, you will pay more attention to
> where you put them, or you will assign them
> a special place where you can easily find
> them and make a habit of placing them
> there regularly.
>
> If you prepare for misunderstandings and for
> doing something difficult together, you will
> communicate more clearly and kindly.
>
> If you prepare for hunger/crabbiness, you
> will keep snacks on hand.

C. **When anger happens in response to frequent ignoring or lack of cooperation.** If you've tended to get angry with others because they haven't typically listened or cooperated with you:

1. Talk to the person/people about this.

   a. Ask them what you might do to adjust and gain their ear so they can listen/or cooperate with you.

   b. Tell them you will be willing to continue to listen and cooperate with them, as they are willing to listen and cooperate with you.

2. Consider doing something different than usual, that gets their attention. Surprise them with a gift or special act of service or outing.

3. Try speaking the love language of the other person.

   If you have spoken their love language and they continue to show little to no interest in speaking yours, try telling them you will do x, or won't do x, if they continue to disrespect you. Then follow through with your warning.

D. If someone frequently gets snippy with you and this causes you anger:

1. Ask the person about their expectations, such as their likes/dislikes/preferences
2. Establish Boundaries or Rules – Write them down for reference. This will establish peace, trust, and enjoyment.
3. Communicate your needs/concerns
4. Look for and negotiate win/win solutions.
   a. Focus on the goal of each person.
   b. Find a way that's acceptable to both of you. (There are usually multiple ways of doing things.) Take turns, if needed.
   c. Ask for help, if necessary.

Forgiveness

Is it ok to get angry? **Yes**, but do not let the anger stay for long, so you don't become bitter.

Forgiveness is another way we can deal with anger. It is a choice. Forgiveness sets us and the other person free. If we remember this, it will help us to move past an offense by acknowledging it and then choosing to forget it.

Does forgiveness mean allowing someone to hurt us over and over? No.

What would help you forgive someone?

Is there anyone who has hurt you that you would like an apology from?

What would you like them to say or do to help you forgive them?

Should you feel bad about expecting someone to acknowledge/change their behavior? No.

Should you feel bad about asking them?   No.

Have they already apologized, but not in the way you expected or were hoping for?

How to Forgive Someone Else?

First, think the best of the other person. Remember everyone makes mistakes.

Secondly, go to the person and tell them what they did that hurt you. If it's severe or has happened often, feel free to ask them to do something to help make up for the offense – to help you forgive them and help them not repeat the behavior.

Restitution

> -Repayment when damages have occurred

> -May be necessary in cases of blatant disrespect or when damages are severe.

Benefits of Restitution

> - Increases learning of correct behavior

> - Increases respect

> - Increases right behavior

When we are hurting in our attempt to love someone else, things are out of balance. We are loving our neighbor more than ourselves, not as ourselves.

Tips for Dealing with Unmet Expectations

1. Perceive/Acknowledge Good in the Other Person

> -Try thinking from the other person's point of view.

> -Think of their feelings/needs

> -Think of their challenges/experiences

> -Check it out before jumping to conclusions

2. Eliminate words like; should, always, and never. They imply judgment. Instead use words like; sometimes, often, and rarely. They seem more

truthful and will help with understanding, acceptance, and cooperation.

*It is usually in our best interest to choose to forgive and forget the offense, regardless of their behavior, to save ourselves from bitterness.

Here is a review of the communication formulas we can follow to help deal with negative emotions and overcome challenges:

2 Step Communication Formula:

> *I'm feeling _____.*
>
> *I need _____.*

4 Step Communication Formula:

> *"I feel _____ (feeling word). "*
>
> *"I like when_____."*
>
> *"I need or would like _____."*
>
> *"Would you be willing to _____?"*

4 Step Communication Example 1

1. *"**I feel** frustrated."*
2. *"**I like when** the house is kept clean because it helps me function better and experience less anxiety."*

3. *"**I need** help keeping the house clean."*
4. *"**Would you be willing to** put things back where they belong? Or **would you be willing to** help me establish a home for certain items that we can agree on?"*

4 step Communication – Example 2

1. *"**I feel** sad."*
2. *"**I like when** you think the best of me."*
3. *"**I need** understanding."*
4. *"**Would you be willing to** listen to understand what I am saying?"*

Response Examples

"Yes, I need some time to calm down and get something to eat first."

"Do you mind if we talk about this after supper? That will help me listen better."

Communication Strategy in Reverse

*"**Would you mind** if I ask you a question about your plans?"*

*"**I like when I know your plans.***

*"**I feel** included and not anxious, when I know your plans."*

It's also a good idea to check out what the other person is thinking and feeling.

"I'm thinking you are thinking ____ *about* ____ .

    Is that what you're thinking?"

"I'm thinking you are feeling ____ *about* ____ .

    Is that what you're feeling?"

"I'm thinking you are saying or needing ____ .

    Am I correct?"

Another way to check things out w/example

    "I see you ____ *(pulling your hair)".*

    "I hear _____ *(the frustration in your voice)."*

    "I think you might need ____ *(a break)."*

    "Is that what you need?"

Checking with the other person about what they are thinking and feeling, helps to minimize misunderstanding and reduces the occurrence of negative feelings, or more negative feelings.

It's also important to create effective thought patterns for reaching your goals and optimal health. Choosing the thoughts you think, will help to manage the emotions of yourself and others.

Next are some examples of thought patterns that can help to manage negative emotions.

Thoughts to conquer challenges

I am responsible for my thoughts, and responses.

I speak well of others and practice positive self-talk.

I am understanding and kind.

I allow others to be who they are.

I'm responsible for my life and choices and I allow others to do the same.

I let go of hurts, allow myself to grieve, and move forward.

I think before I respond. I communicate clearly.

I ask for what I want and need with ease.

I think about what I am thankful for.

I serve others when I can do so with a smile.

I open myself to humor, friendship, and love.

I seek and attract mutually satisfying relationships with family and friends.

I create win/win solutions with others.

Relationship Difficulties

Unfortunately, we have all learned unhealthy ways of interacting with others and unhealthy ways of getting what we want. The following information will help couples connect and conquer challenges.

How to Stop Unhealthy Reactions/Interactions

Step 1 **Awareness** – usually produces humility and leads to forgiveness

■■■■■■■■■■■■■■■■■■■■■■■■■■■■■■■■■■

Step 2 **Knowing** how to de-escalate and prevent future fighting

■■■■■■■■■■■■■■■■■■■■■■■■■■■■■■■■■■

Step 3 **Changing** your own behavior to get the desired result

■■■■■■■■■■■■■■■■■■■■■■■■■■■■■■■■■■

Approximately 35 years ago after getting out of a dysfunctional seven-year long relationship, I attended a class created by Paul Hegstrom and taught by Dixie Carter. The class was called Learning to Live - Learning to Love. It was a class created to reduce domestic violence and help heal individuals from all kinds of abuse, including emotional, physical, and spiritual abuse. I learned many things in the 12-week course. One of the most valuable pieces of information included Dirty Fighting Techniques. Little did I know, but I was a habitual user of several of them. I soon realized it is common for all of us to have habits we are unaware of. Once the awareness comes, behavior can be changed. What an eye-opening experience it was for me!

We all learn undesired ways of interacting that can make situations worse and more complicated, instead of better. Awareness is the key. Until one is aware of what they are doing and knows how to change it, they probably will continue the behavior.

Since affirmations can be used to reprogram the subconscious mind and respond differently to each other or change our own behaviors, I have added specific affirmations to the common fighting scenarios below.

Fighting will lessen over time and becomes less severe as they are applied. Don't get discouraged. Keep working at it. You will get there!

· ·

What to do when someone gives you the silent treatment: Tell them you would like to discuss subject_____. Ask them when a good time would be for them to be willing to discuss _____ with you.

What to do when someone blames you: First, acknowledge and take responsibility for your own behavior and how it contributed to the problem.

Second, kindly ask the other person to acknowledge what aspect of their behavior contributed to the problem.

What to do when someone bullies you: Ask them if they can think of a way in which both of you can get something you both want.

Affirmation to stop bullying: ***We create win/win solutions!"***

What to do when someone complains of more than one thing at a time? Tell the other person you feel overwhelmed and need to discuss one issue at a time, so you can properly address their concerns.

Affirmation: *"**We discuss one issue at a time** (when it happens), **at our established talk time.** Also, "**That was then, this is now!**"* will help stick to the present issue.

What to do when someone demands answers? Acknowledge the other person's disappointment, first. Second, you may ask the other person to tell you how they are feeling.

Affirmation to stop demands: *"**I realize things will not always turn out the way I expect them to**."* Instead of using the word "**why**", as in *"Why were you late?"* Try stating for example, *"I am wondering what happened that you were later than expected."*

What to do when someone is frustrated with you? Acknowledge the other person's feelings of frustration. Be willing to tell the other person your willingness to make efforts to adjust your behavior in the future.

What to do when someone says they are going to do something equally as wrong because you did something? First, acknowledge past hurtful behavior of your own. Second, ask the other person to take responsibility for their own actions, as well.

What to do when someone leaves: Wait a while. When they return, ask them if they're ready to discuss the issue. If they are not, acknowledge their feelings of hesitation or fear in addressing the issue. Ask them when they might be willing to discuss it, or if they think it would be better to discuss it via writing.

Affirmation to stop leaving: *"If I need time to calm down or to think, I can ask for twenty minutes to collect my thoughts and tell the other person I will be ready to discuss it then. I can write down my thoughts to the other person if I think it will help one or both of us."* *If I need a longer time to process or calm down, I can ask the other person for it and tell them when I think I might be able to discuss the subject."* This will lessen anxiety.

What to do when someone calls you a name:
Acknowledge your own feelings of disrespect and
ask the person to tell you how they are feeling, in a
respectful way.

**What to do when a person says, *"You will never
change:"*** Acknowledge the other person's feelings
and address concerns. Request the other person to
express their concerns and expect you to do your
best to find mutually agreeable solutions in the
future.

**When a person is sarcastic and then implies
something is wrong with you for how you
heard a complaint**: Tell the other person what
you think they might be thinking and how they
might be feeling. Ask them if you are correct.
Secondly, you can simply ask the person to tell you
how they feel in the future and assure them you
care about them and their needs.

**When someone implies there should be a
breakup:** First, acknowledge the other person's
frustration/needs, as well as your own. Remember,
everyone can change. You can ask the other person
if they would be willing to do what is needed, in
exchange for something else.

**When a person starts an argument at a bad
time:** Remember to have or ask for discussions at
times of the day that work for both people. Tell the

person you would like to discuss the issue at a better time. Suggest an alternative time to discuss the matter. This will help reduce anxiety for both people.

What to do when a person implies, they are better than the other for some reason? Agree with any true statements the other person makes and remind the other person that your view, needs, and contributions are important too. Then ask the other person to find a win/win solution, in which both of you are at least 75% satisfied.

When someone ignores the other: Remember, if it's not a good time for you or the other person to listen, arrangements can be made for another specific time to listen to or discuss a topic. Do your best to approach each other in ways and at times that are convenient for both of you.

When someone is holding a grudge: Ask or tell what can be done to help with forgiveness of the past. Remind each other to look forward and concentrate on positive changes and efforts

When someone is compared to another person they don't like or are angry with: Acknowledge there may be some similarities and acknowledge the other person's frustration and/or anxiety. Also, take responsibility for your own attitudes and behavior. *Affirm: "I would not like to be*

*compared in negative ways to others.
Therefore, I will not do it to anyone else."*

What to do when words like "always," "every," "all," and "never" are used in an argument:
When used against you, tell the other person it is difficult for you to respond to exaggeration. Ask them to instead use words like "often," "seldom," "sometimes," "rarely," etc. because it helps you to respond better. Then address their concern.

Note: Using the word "BUT" negates what a person said prior to the word "but".

Silly example: "I love you, <u>but</u> you drive me crazy!" **(Versus)** "I love you <u>&</u> you drive me crazy!"

*Affirm: "**Others will listen to me much better when I use the word "AND."***

*The above list of unhealthy interactions was derived from a dirty fighting list from Paul Hegstrom's work at Life Skills International. The affirmations and responses to stop unhealthy reactions/Interactions are my own. Another unhealthy interaction is the use of guilt.

When a person tries to make another feel guilty: This is usually done when the person wants some type of acknowledgment, an apology a thank you, or maybe even cooperation. **Ask the other person what the guilt is about and what it is**

they need. They probably don't realize they are using guilt.

Another source of fighting is when different words have different meanings to different people. For example: Within the first 4 years of being married, my husband and I got into some arguments over number words. Upon further questioning, I realized we had different meanings for the same words. He learned somewhere that the word "few" meant 2-3. And the word "several" meant 3-4. Whereas I learned the word "few" meant 4-5, and "several" meant 6-8. This difference can be confusing and important when discussing a "few" hundred or "several hundred" dollars – if you know what I mean. When something doesn't sound right, remember to check it and the other person's frame of reference out.

General Affirmations for Healthy Interactions

"I take responsibility for my own feelings, attitudes, and behaviors."

"I think the best of others and treat them with the respect I would want to be treated with."

"If someone does or says something I don't like, I can ask them to simply tell me why they are upset. I then can ask for what they need.

"I acknowledge and discuss concerns with others."
"If I need time to think before responding, I ask for time to gather my thoughts to present/address concerns as needed (and in writing, if necessary)."

The Past

Past relationships, and the history of a current relationship, can be the most difficult challenge to conquer for connecting.

Two simple affirmations that can bring healing from the past and leave it behind, are:

"I forgive and let it go!   That was then, and this is now!"

Anger and unforgiveness are often the culprits of the past. We might be angry about hurtful things that have been said or done. Or, we might be angry about important things that were not said or were not done.

Anger in and of itself is not bad. It really is a signal of disappointment or an unmet expectation. Please see the previous section on frustration and anger.

According to Paul Hegstrom, in his "Learning to Live - Learning to Love" class, anger is a secondary emotion; meaning it's precipitated by another emotion such as sadness, embarrassment, frustration, or fear.

Anger becomes problematic when it gets out of hand or when we fail to acknowledge our feelings. It's okay to become angry.

Forgiveness is a way we can deal with anger - anger at ourselves and anger at others. It's important to acknowledge our feelings so we can deal with things in a healthy manner rather than let them eat at us and cause sickness in body and relationships.

Telling ourselves the truth about ourselves, others, or a situation, **can help us let go of anger and forgive.**

As we choose to forgive, we are set free. Forgiveness is a loving attitude with limits. Forgiveness sets us and the other person free emotionally. It is loving our neighbor as ourselves; **not** more than ourselves.

We don't have to feel bad when <u>we</u> expect acknowledgment of and changes in behavior or attitudes from others. It is okay to have expectations. Set limits and establish guidelines to follow. It makes things clear, so everyone knows the rules. It helps to play fair, so the involved persons can enjoy the game, so to speak.

How to forgive when it keeps hurting?

Set limits and reward good behavior only!

Restitution can help with forgiving, as well as acceptance/appreciation of forgiveness when someone continues the undesired behavior after they know it is problematic.

It's okay to ask for repayment when damages have occurred, so learning takes place, and the behavior stops. It is also okay to ask for some type of restitution when damages are severe, or someone has broken the law. This is many times necessary because the person had no regard for the law or for their fellow being. Restitution will help in teaching correct behavior and in serving justice.

Occasionally, one may need to end a toxic relationship. It's okay. We don't have to be close to everyone. We are just supposed to love them as we love ourselves. If we are hurting ourselves in our attempt to love them, we are unbalanced. This is not God's will. Love is a choice and so is forgiveness. They are gifts. Make every attempt to get along and cooperate with others whenever possible. Do what you can. When you cannot cooperate, say "No," and pray for them. **Apologies can help with forgiveness.** *Although, if an apology is given in a way the other person does not value, it may only make things worse!*

How do I forgive?

1. Pray for the person each day. Ask God to help and bless them.
2. Write down what you are having trouble forgiving them for, specifically. Include something you need them to say or do that helps you to forgive them.
3. Ask them to read your writing. Thank them for taking the time to read it, as you give it to them.
4. If they do not respond within a reasonable time frame, ask them to tell you in their own words why you were upset and how you felt.

Knowing your significant other understands how you were feeling, will help you to forgive. Also, knowing how they felt at the time and why, will help too. Acknowledge how they must have been feeling. This will help them to forgive you.

Remember, until they learn otherwise, the other person will tend to apologize in the way they value (because they are trying to love you the way they know how); which might be very different from the way you apologize. The motive is the same, however! Both people usually want to repair and have a better relationship. Just because it's not done in the way you want it, doesn't mean it isn't sincere.

What to do when I have hurt, offended, or neglected my spouse?

Here are some examples of things to say:

1. *"You have put up with this for far too long!"*
2. *"I don't blame you for being upset!"*
3. *"I understand how you would feel _____!"*

    (Be sure to acknowledge the feeling.)

    *You can lovingly look in their eyes, hold their hand, hug or give them some space and stay nearby and be accepting. You might take a break and let the apology soak in. **There is usually one person in the relationship that needs a longer time to process and feel the apology.***

Importantly, you can apologize in the way they value it. Acknowledge how they must have been feeling. You might ask how you can make it up to them and then do your best to follow through. **You can use the Relationship Map for Happiness at the beginning of this book to learn what kind and method of apology your spouse values.** This should ensure an effective apology and acceptance of your apology.

Typically, one person values a simple "I'm sorry" rather than an "I'm sorry and an explanation, while the other person values an explanation with the "I'm sorry. Both well-meaning individuals may offend the other – purely because they don't value the way it is done. *Ask the other person what sincere apologies look, and sound like, to them. Then, when you apologize to them, apologize in that way.* Things will go much smoother!

Consider presenting apologies via writing, in addition to verbally. This will allow for re-reading and processing time.

Secrets/Siding with Others

Keeping secrets from the other person and siding with other family members causes disconnect between couples. How many times has a mother sided with a son or a father sided with a daughter because of the harshness of the other parent? This has led to betrayal and suffering.

It is when the mother and father take responsibility for their actions and work together as a team, that unity, reoccurring peace, and connections happen.

We are the creators of unity and peace in our world. As we take responsibility for our actions and attitudes, and see and believe ourselves, and others to be "good," peace is created.

Eliminate secrets between husband/child – against wife. And **eliminate secrets between wife/child** – against the husband.

Secrets breed contempt, resentment, and dissention!

It is when we blame each other and try to cover up our own defects that it causes shame, discontent, and resentment.

As we listen to each other and address the concerns of all, while staying within the established boundaries, it is then that we create strong connections and reoccurring peace:

1. Search for the good in each other
2. Honor yourself and the other person as valuable and unique.
3. Listen to understand
4. Speak the truth in love.
5. Cooperate, when you can.
6. Communicate concerns.
7. Share what you have and know.
8. Use your tongue to heal, restore, and give life to the other!

Chapter 5
Building Unity

Building unity is essential in couples connecting. Sharing power and control is something that couples frequently struggle with. For couples with a religious background, the following information can help with obtaining a closer connection.

If we view marriage as a team, in which the husband is the coach and the wife is the assistant coach, *it might make things easier to comprehend and help keep scripture in proper perspective and balance.*

For example: Although a coach has final decision-making authority, an effective coach will rely on an assistant coach's knowledge and listen to their assistant's concerns, prior to making major decisions. Likewise, an effective assistant coach will support the decisions of the coach and respect the coach as the leader. Problems happen in marriages when the assistant tries to be the coach or when the coach doesn't take the lead or when the coach is not listening to the needs and concerns of the team. *It is much easier for the assistant coach to respect and follow the coach's lead when she feels listened to.*

It is also easier if both individuals view the playbook each day. Keeping the "Holy" book on the kitchen table makes it easy to consult and read the team playbook. A daily scripture reading and prayer at mealtime, helps couples get along and work together in unity as a team.

Further, in Emerson Eggerichs', book <u>Love and Respect</u>, he says **men value respect more than love and women value love more than respect.** *Because of this, a man might have difficulty doing something his wife tells him to do; especially if it's said or done in a way he perceives as disrespectful and controlling.*

I have found over time, that women may do/say something they themselves perceive as loving, such as helping a man find a parking spot. Most generally, men perceive this as disrespectful and controlling, since they are perfectly capable of finding their own parking spot.

Likewise, a man may not open a woman's car door because he is trying to show respect in that she is perfectly capable of opening her own door. However, a woman may perceive it as unloving.

So, it depends on each person and what they perceive as respectful or loving. It also depends on if it's a man or a woman. In the love/respect section of my Relationship Map for Happiness, couples can find out what each person views as loving and respectful. It helps take the hurt and fight out of everyday situations.

Unity or Team Building for Couples in General

For unity it is important for couples to agree to disagree when they cannot agree and to m**ake decisions based on the goals and concerns of each other.** If it's important to one person, it's ultimately important to the other.

As couples take turns making decisions and/or letting the person who has more expertise in an area make the final decisions regarding those things, this can be helpful. For instance, the person with mechanical experience can handle the items regarding car maintenance or house maintenance and the person who is relationship-oriented can handle the social types of things, such as planning with friends, etc. This is just a general guideline. **Do what you are good at and enjoy doing.** Default the other things to the other person. At times, try to grow by doing things you are uncomfortable with, if it's important to the other person or if it's a job or activity neither of you like - such as folding laundry.

On activities neither of you like, take turns. This will help keep fighting at bay and build a sense of teamwork, appreciation, and peace.

Remember to appreciate, thank, and reward each other for jobs well done.

For couples who are very competitive, try playing a game each day so you can get your competitive needs taken care of, and not have the need to compete within the relationship itself.

Handling Finances

Finances are often an issue among couples; especially when there are limited resources or one of them has a spending problem. Spending issues can sometimes indicate bipolar disorder. Once it is adequately treated, usually with a mood stabilizer, decision-making abilities usually improve, and spending is normalized. Life then can be much smoother.

Because money can be a dividing force for many couples, I've recommended to most couples a **mutual checking and savings accounts to pay mutual bills and save for the team.** This eliminates fighting over who is paying for what. I've also recommended **each person have their own additional separate savings account**; in which the same percentage of each of their own income goes into it. This way, they each have access to a portion of the money that they do not have to have the other person's approval to spend. It is nice to have it to use when there is something one person may want, which is something the other may not agree to (or to use when one wants to surprise the other with a gift of some kind). For spouses who work at home and raise the kids, I suggest they get the same percentage from the household income as the money-earning spouse does, to put in their savings account.

This might seem like an impossible task at times; especially when resources are limited. A small percentage such as 2-5% of the household income can add up and give each spouse some independence and freedom – even if it only allows them to buy their favorite coffee each week.

I have found the spiritual practice of tithing or giving 10% percent of the household income to the church or to help others, is a practice that ends up helping the overall financial situation. It has helped me to not worry as much about finances. It seems although it may be a sacrifice to give it at times, the better the financial situation seems to be, in general.

If both individuals do not agree on tithing 10%, do not let this be a source of contention. Instead, consider mutually deciding on a percentage of income you **are** willing to give to others. Or consider tithing a given percentage to others and the same given percentage to the spouse who may not support giving that said percentage of the household income to others. That way they too can see some return for the hard work they do and won't be resentful.

If you cannot mutually agree **on a percentage to give to others, decide what you will give from your own income and let the other person give from their income what they want to give.**

As far as other practices go, it is imperative to **agree on an amount of money that is safe to spend at any given time, without the pre-approval of the other person, and then don't spend more than that amount.** This will keep peace and build trust and unity. **Agree that purchases over the agreed spending amount need prior discussion and approval of the other.** This allows for some freedom in spending.

The other advice I have for handling finances is for **the person that is better at money management, to be the one to pay the bills.** If both individuals are capable, the one who can handle the stress associated with money the best should be the one to make sure the bills are paid. If both individuals are capable and can handle the stress, consider taking turns each year or paying the bills together, to give each other a break. **If neither person is good at money management, consider a trusted person to be a payee.** Whoever pays the monthly bills, will want to keep the other person informed of the current financial situation by sharing bill amounts and bank balances with the other. This helps to make sure both individuals understand, trust, and work together as a team. It eliminates the tendency to fight about finances.

Also, do not hesitate to seek out financial experts or consultants as needed.

Disciplining Children

Children are a wonderful, yet they can really stress out a relationship. This is especially true when there are step-kids involved. **Dr. Matthew A. Johnson** created a brilliant method for dealing with discipline fairly and consistently regardless of which kid it is or, who's kid it is. It helps the parents stay on the same team and eliminates fighting due to different parenting styles.

His method is called "Family Rules." You can learn more by reading his book <u>Positive Parenting with a Plan: Family Rules Book</u> at www.family-rules.com.

My brief explanation/rendition of <u>his</u> method is the following:

1. Parents agree to and write out the rules for the family, to be posted and understood by all. (i.e., no hitting or swearing, etc.)

2. Parents also write out numerous recipe cards with age-appropriate activities on them. Activities can range from dusting the living room, to reading a book to a sibling.

3. Parents also include a few "Grace" cards with the other activity cards and assemble, in a shuffled order, in a recipe card box.

4. When a member (adults included) breaks a rule, they are to immediately pull a card from the front of the box, read it, and do the activity the card displays on it; whether it's in word or picture form. Cards are to be returned to the back of the box. If a "Grace" card is drawn, no activity is required.

I have found a motivation jar with things like money, candy, or pieces of paper with things written on them (like a trip for ice cream or a ballgame) can be used when a family member has not had to pull a card for a desired length of time. It reinforces desired behavior and encourages teamwork.

The purpose of pulling cards is to get the person's attention off doing the undesired activities, and on to doing more appropriate activities. If family members enjoy pulling and doing cards, that is okay. It will keep them from doing undesired behavior and at the very least, will keep the house cleaner.

This method also keeps parents from having to constantly figure out discipline choices, especially during times of busyness or stress. It keeps discipline consistent and in balance. It keeps discipline fair among all family members and avoids issues of jealousy and resentment. It keeps parents from judging each other and/or arguing about discipline. It's easy to implement and ensures that discipline happens and happens in a non-abusive way. It's a brilliant idea because it is a win/win solution to a historically major dilemma.

Chore Distribution

Another disconnect for couples can be chore distribution. Dishes and laundry are the major concerns, because of their daily volume and repetitive nature. The person responsible for these tasks often becomes overloaded, burdened, and resentful when it is their sole responsibility to do them; especially when they have a job outside of the home.

Since everyone produces, I suggest all members of the family take part in doing the tasks. Not only will it help with family relationships, but it will also help members become responsible/functioning adults when they have their own houses/families to manage.

Of course, it depends on the number of people in the family. Each person can be responsible for some part of doing laundry and dishes daily. Children as young as 2 or 3 should be able to help get the laundry to the basket and their dishes to the dishwasher. This is how I suggest tasks be divided.

Dishes

It is helpful for all family members to pick up their own dishes after eating and take them to the dishwasher. In addition to this, each person can be assigned a responsibility based on interest and skill level. Larger families can have one person put condiments in the refrigerator, another person wipe off the table and the counters, another person wash the pots and the pans, another sweep the floor, and another take out the trash.

Making a habit of one person always emptying the dishwasher each morning and perhaps the same person starting the dishwasher every night, allows family members an empty dishwasher each day to add dishes to it - as they are dirtied, during the day.

It is also helpful to make a habit of emptying the kitchen trash every night when starting the dishwasher.

Laundry

Over the years, I have found it easiest to manage laundry when a habit is made for someone in the family to start a load of laundry each morning. If another family member makes a habit of changing the loads when they come home from school or work, it is very helpful. Folding laundry can be done when a member or members watch a favorite TV show in the evening. Each person can be responsible for collecting their pile of things, taking them to their rooms, and putting them away at night. If you have members of your family who do not like putting away their clothes, and you have one person who likes it (and is good at it), that can be their job. Each family member can be responsible for getting laundry to the designated laundry collection site each day.

*When dishes or laundry or any other tasks seem overwhelming and out of control, I have found it best to start with the easiest task and then follow with the next, easiest task. It helps to gain momentum. For instance, the easiest task may begin with throwing a Kleenex or other trash away. **Looking for the easiest and most doable thing and then*** *doing it, will help to get the job done, rather than focusing on the mountain of work.*

Creating an Environment of Cooperation and Teamwork

The phrases below work like magic in cooperation and teamwork, with men especially, because they perceive them as respectful. Women, children, and teenagers like them too.

"Do you mind if _____?" and

"Would you be willing to _____?"

"I value your contribution." Or "Thank you so much for, _____!"

Using words like please, although it's polite, can make the other person feel as though they should comply or like they have little choice in the matter.

You will tend to get more honest answers to your questions, and greater cooperation, with the above phrases.

Affirmations that help with Teamwork and Negotiations:

1. **We work together as a team.**
2. **We create win/win solutions**

Negotiation Strategies

Cooperation helps couples to get things accomplished that they could not do independently. Cooperation through negotiation creates peace and connection.

When negotiating, it's important to negotiate at a time that works for both persons. Negotiating time can be established by asking the question: *"When is a good time for you to discuss _____?"*

At the agreed-upon time, it's important to keep the question: "How can we both get what we want?"

When negotiating; identify the problem, list concerns, establish goals, and brainstorm solutions. These can be done via discussion or via writing. When topics are especially "hot," writing may be the preferred method.

> An example of using this to address a housing issue:

> Your feelings/concerns about the house?
> _____
> 1.
>
> 2.
>
> 3.

Your goals regarding the house?

    1.

    2.

    <u>My ideas for addressing the house are:</u>

    1.

    2.

Key things to keep in mind when negotiating:

1. Take care of any other unfinished business of the past, if possible, prior to negotiations. This helps with cooperation and fosters positive attitudes.
2. Keep in mind the question, "How can we both get something we want, and/or need?"
3. Agree whenever possible.
4. Give credit to the other when they have a good idea.
5. It is important to remember each person is different and will look at things differently. To expect 100% agreement is unrealistic.
6. Remember: Don't be offended if the other person doesn't embrace your first solution.
7. You can trade: "Will you do X for me, if I do X for you?"
8. 75-90% satisfaction goal; in which, unless both/all parties are not 75-90% satisfied with the outcome, the deal is not equitable, and

another solution is sought. In polar-opposite situations, neither person will be 100% happy with the outcome. However, if both are relatively and equally happy with the outcome (at least 75-90% happy with it) it's a win/win solution.

Phrases to use when negotiating may include phrases such as:

"It bothers me when _____*," "Is it ok if I get* _____*, in exchange for* _____*."*

Examples of Negotiated Agreements:

Situation: Bill hates cleaning the bathroom and Nancy cleans bathrooms for a living. Nancy would like a break from cleaning the bathroom at home.

Negotiated Solution: Bill happily cleans the bathroom 1-2 times a month at home in exchange for Nancy to bake the cookies from the mixes Bill buys at the store.

Situation: Joe has had a history of being treated poorly by certain members of Cathy's family. Cathy wants Joe to attend important family functions like holiday gatherings, birthdays, etc.

Negotiated Solution: Whenever there is a family event, Joe and Cathy will drive separately. Joe congratulates the person being celebrated and talks with family who treat him well. He leaves after a brief appearance to go help a friend in need, which he honestly arranges prior to each event. This way Cathy is not left to make up some excuse as to why Joe leaves family functions early. Cathy is happy he is involved, and Joe is happy he doesn't have to be in uncomfortable situations in which he has no control. Joe looks like the good guy he is to family members because he showed up and helps friends.

Situation: Carol and Larry love to entertain. They have two young children. Carol loves to plan, and Larry loves to plan and execute. Both enjoy family time with their own parents. Carol does not like spending time with Larry's Mom because Larry's Mom does not like her and is often rude to her in front of others. Because of this, Carol feels her mother-in-law ruins every holiday and birthday with her family. They do not want to celebrate a birthday more than once or a holiday more than once with family members.

Negotiated Solution: Birthday parties for the children are celebrated at their own roomy house where they can make food and decorate as they want. Birthday guests alternate each year between Larry's parents and Carol's parents. In the year in which Larry's parents come to the birthday of the oldest child, Carol's parents will come to the birthday of the youngest child in the same year. The next year it will be flipped. Since both Larry and Carol like planning parties, Larry plans the parties for those celebrated with his parents and Carol plans the parties for those celebrated with her parents. Since it is so difficult to get time off from work, holiday time must be scheduled way in advance. Holiday gatherings will be alternated between her family and his. If one family visits for Christmas this year, the other family visits for Christmas the following year. This solution ensures fairness and equality in time spent with the Grandchildren. It gives them more control, and less confusion. It allows equality in planning gatherings. Larry agreed to help execute the parties Carol plans - decreasing her stress and giving her opportunities to spend time with her family when they visit. Likewise, Carol will help execute Larry's plans when his family visits. This gives her the opportunity to stay busy and not have to interact as much with Larry's Mom. They both can shine and have their own desires met when their own families visit. This allows the enjoyment of their families, without fighting afterward.

Chapter 6

Creating Peace

When it comes to couples connecting, there are other things couples can do to create reoccurring peace within their lives.

Here are some basic things to remember when interacting with each other.

An imbalance of power contributes to problems among us.

Within the traditional relationship of one man and one woman, if something is important to the woman, it's important for the man to listen to the woman, consider it and make some sort of provision for her concern. If something is important to the man, it is important for her to pay attention to his concern and cooperate and help him the best she can. Likewise, in a non-traditional relationship, it's important to listen to each other. Also, if something is important to a child, it is important for parents to listen and learn and make sure the child's needs/concerns are met.

All are important! All have different functions, abilities, and positions.

It is in unity that we stand! A unified house (family) listens to each other and has lasting peace. The love is true and not counterfeit. **If one person's needs are deemed as more important than the others, on a regular basis, problems**

are sure to come. Peace comes at a cost and is short-lived in these situations.

When all needs/concerns as a family are provided for and met, lasting peace and love are present.

We create lasting peace when we listen to understand, look for the good in each other, and work together to address each other's concerns.

If we ignore ourselves in the process, we self-destruct too! We become out of balance and get counterfeit peace lasting for only a short period.

When we equally listen, consider, provide for, and address all concerns - This is when we have lasting peace!

Additionally, if a Husband is harsh/offensive with a woman's child, the woman feels the same as if he was that way with her. She will tend to be offended and resent it until the man repairs the relationship with the child – And perhaps vice versa. The man may resent the woman in the same scenario until the woman makes things right with his child.

The fighting will probably continue until the relationship with the child/ren is repaired. Men, acknowledge the hurt to both her and her child! It would be helpful for the woman to acknowledge any of her or her child's disobedience to the man's word and the hurt that is done to him, as well. This is when more lasting peace will come!

Practices for Peaceful Connection

Understanding/Acceptance

Perceiving the good in self and others

Accuracy in speech

Appreciation/Acknowledgement

Accepting/Including

Agreeing/Cooperating

Listening

Honesty/Humility

Respect/Honor

Causes of Difficulty

Lack of Communication

Perceiving the bad in self and others

Overgeneralizing/Exaggerating

Judging/Blaming

Excluding/Ignoring

Interrupting/Jumping to conclusions

Taking the other for granted

Threatening

Name calling

Lying

Communication with each other seeks connection with each other. It's taking interest in each other. Communication can be either peace-creating and help us connect or it can cause difficulties.

When we look for the good in each other it helps us to get along better and feel more at peace.

As we seek to understand and accept each other and take responsibility for ourselves and our communications with each other, we also create peace.

If we look for the good in each other and use accurate **words/speech like:**

> You sometimes...   You often...
>
> You rarely...   Many people...
>
> I often...   I sometimes....

Statements like these are usually more accurate/true. They can be easier to respond appropriately to and will help with honest and peaceful communication.

They can help us to listen and hear what each other is saying, help us to adjust our speech, and to get along more peacefully.

Absolute thinking and overgeneralizations can cause problems among us. They are usually untrue. Examples of such are; using words like always, and never as in "I never..." or "You always..." or other absolutes such as, "Everyone is..."

Appreciating and acknowledging each other creates peace and helps us connect.

Being *thankful* creates peace within us and helps us to be more pleasant to be around. It also helps us to appreciate each other and connect more.

Love/Acceptance (towards self and others) creates peace and happiness among us.

Saying:

    -Words of praise and acceptance

    -Words of acknowledgment of effort

    -Words of thanksgiving

    -Acknowledgment of the others' feelings

Showing:

    -Smile, hug, kiss, or holding hands

    -Being together (enjoying, listening cooperating)

    -Doing something nice – serving the other

    -Giving a gift (what hey value, want/need)

    -Self-discipline (doing what you say you will do)

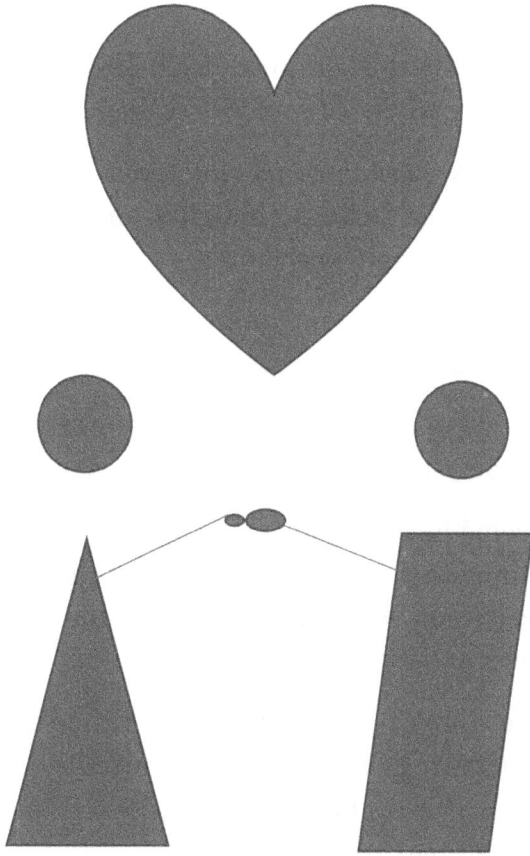

Creating win/win situations/solutions with each other creates peace.

As we speak the truth with each other and cooperate when we can, we create peace.

As we ask questions in loving tones and acknowledge feelings, thoughts, and situations, we create even more peace.

As we keep judgment, guilt, and blame out of communication we create peace.

Agreeing only when we can truly agree and keep our word, leads to more lasting reoccurring peace.

Agreeing just to agree, while in our hearts or minds planning to do something different than what we agreed upon, will cause problems, and creates counterfeit and temporary peace.

As we go to each other with an attitude of peace, remembering that we all make mistakes, we avoid fights with each other and can stand firm in whatever may come against us.

As we adjust our thinking and speech, the landscape around us changes.

Accepting Responsibility for our thinking and speech will change our lives in the direction we desire.

Ways to show appreciation to and connect with each other are as follows:

Show appreciation

Make a special dinner

Share a gift, serve favorite cookies, sing a song, or give a foot massage.

"Thank you!" (With a hug, ice cream, or card)

"Brenda said she liked your spaghetti. And so, did I!" (w/a smile)

"I love you!" (w/ a kiss, emoji, love note)

"You are so kind to me. You encourage me when I am sad. You charge my cell phone without me asking. You call the doctor when I am sick." (With a smile, hug, or gift)

Including Others

"How can I help? What do you need?"

"I want to share my ____ with you."

"What are you up to?"

What to do when you have a disagreement or disagree with someone:

1. Agree with what you can agree on.

2. You might agree to disagree. Or agree to give it some time before discussing again.

Try thinking: "I look for something I can agree with/or help with."

1. I acknowledge the other person's feelings and needs and tell them what I heard them say or what I understand them to need.

2. I say what I'm willing to do and do it.

3. If I am unable or I am unwilling to help, I say so. It's ok to say "No," when I need to.

Verbally recognize their importance to you,
   "You are my best friend."

Verbally Recognize talents, knowledge, interests, efforts & challenges

"You do _ __ well." "I like your sense of humor."

"This is your area of expertise."

"You worked hard on that project."

"You were successful in maneuvering around the challenges you faced."

Cooperating

How?   *Show/Tell*

"You look, and sound stressed. Is there anything I can do to help?"

"You said you needed ... I am ordering it for you."

"You look cold. Would you like me to turn up the heat?"

"You said this was important. Do you have time to do this now? I am willing to do this while you do that, so we can get it done in time."

Imagine yourself in the other's shoes. What might they need? (It will help you be more effective and successful.)

Cooperation – Helps us to get things accomplished that we could not do independently. This creates peace.

Negotiate

1. Listen to and ask about the other person's needs, concerns, and ideas.

2. Consider the other person's needs, concerns, and ideas and state what you understand them to be.

3. State your own needs, concerns, and ideas.

If stating your own concerns and ideas have caused fights in the past, try writing your thoughts down until you are better at verbally communicating and negotiating.

If one person's needs are deemed more important than the others regularly, destruction is sure to come. The peace will be short-lived and come at a cost.

Try your best to negotiate win/win situations and solutions. Take turns. Or agree to disagree.

Listening – helps in our relationships to show we care.

Taking turns, when listening, brings peace.

Men often like directness, with simplicity, in speech. It helps them to focus and follow.

Women like it when feelings are discussed and acknowledged.

> -Consider writing thoughts down to better organize and prepare for more direct and respectful communication.

> -Schedule talk times that are good for all individuals involved.

Seek to understand, before being understood.

<u>These affirmations create peace</u>:

"I listen to understand."

I acknowledge how the other person feels."

"I think before I respond."

Honesty in a relationship helps build a firm foundation of trust. As we trust each other, we connect more easily. This is because we trust the other to speak the truth with us and do what they say they will do. Speaking the truth and doing what we say we will do, is a mark of integrity and character. The practice of such, builds peace and connection within our lives.

Humility repairs relationships. Being able to say, *"I'm sorry. I was wrong"* or *"I made a bad choice,"* initiates connection

Other Practices that lead to peace.

Rest creates peace in our lives. It was discussed earlier in the chapter how sleep affects our relationships. Rest is vitally important.

Keeping too busy can overwhelm us and cause trouble among us. Taking a day each week to rest, reflect and rejuvenate, will help us have more peace within ourselves and our relationships.

Rest means to stop working and sleep or do something enjoyable, such as:

-An outing together, alone, or with a friend

- A car or bike ride, or walk in the woods

-Worship, singing, dancing, or exercising

It gives us strength, enjoyment, a different perspective, and time to reflect and plan.

It helps us be more pleasant to live with - which creates peace.

Honoring the other before yourself is also a practice that will help with connection and lead to more lasting peace within ourselves and our relationships.

*Ask about or check with the other person on what they are feeling and what they need before you tell them what you feel and need.

(If you honor the other person first, the other person will be more open to listening to your feelings and needs.)

If the other person does not respond the way you want or need them to, after you tell them how you are feeling and what you are needing, you can handle the disappointment better because you acknowledged your own feelings and needs.

Chances are things went better for both of you because: 1. You listened to and understood the other person and 2. You stated your needs.

Honoring the other person first helps keep the guesswork out of things. When you honor the other person first, there is less chance for misunderstandings, resentments, and misinterpretation of behavior to occur.

Lastly, listening without interrupting is part of honoring the other person. Even if you have something important to say or if you feel the other person is jumping to conclusions, try your best to wait until your turn to respond.

Chapter 7

Nurturing Connections

For couples to continue to connect, it's important to keep the lines of communication open and ask for what is needed and explain why. A discussion of daily plans is important for making sure everyone understands and knows what to do and what to expect.

An example - *"I need to get the kids to school and finish my presentation, tomorrow morning. Would you be willing and have time to drop the kids off at school tomorrow?"*

Asking the other person about their needs and feelings will also help with connection, satisfaction, and peace.

Sentences like these might be helpful to use during the day:

"What are your plans for tomorrow?' What do you hope to accomplish? Is there anything I can help you with?"

"When is a good time to discuss _____?"

"How can we both get what we want?" "Would you be willing to _____?"

Daily Practices to Nurture Relationship and Maintain Happiness

Here are some ways men and women can nurture their relationships each day.

Daily Ways to Wow Your Woman

1. Ask what she thinks/feels about something and have a conversation about it.
2. Tell her something you like about her each day. *"I like how you _____."*
3. Ask her how you can help her or what you can do to make her life easier and do it.

   Remember these kinds of things
   The *"I love you!"* and *"How was your day, dear?"* *"Is there anything I need to apologize for?"* (When she seems upset with you.)

   "Will you forgive me for _____?" I *understand you felt _____"*

   Tip: When your wife continues over and over about something, try naming her feeling. Saying something like, *"It sounds like you are feeling _____,"* should help her to feel understood and calm down. Then you can redirect (unless she first needs to hear an apology from you) with something like: "Where can I take you for dinner?" Or, you might offer to pray with her or help her with something.

Daily Method to Mesmerize Your Man

1. Touch/or flirt with him to let him know he is desired.
2. Tell/or show him how much you appreciate/respect his efforts to provide for and "Love" you.
3. Ask him if there is something you can do for him to make his life easier or more "enjoyable," and do it.
   Guys like to hear "I love you!" too. They also like to be prayed for.

Schedule **Weekly Date/Alternate Together Time**

It is important to spend specially designated time with each other each week. Having an alternate time, when a babysitter cancels, helps to ensure your special time together is not compromised. Sundays are often a good time to plan and arrange family and dating schedules for the week ahead.

Weekly Communication Connection

Using the communication formats, found in Chapter 2 - Healthy Exchanges, can help ensure that important issues are communicated and handled regularly. Couples can use them at weekly date times to expedite clear/healthy communication. This leaves more time for enjoying fun activities.

Monthly Practices for Nurturing Connections and Creating Happiness

It will help to regularly ask your spouse or anyone else you have a relationship with how things are going for them. **You can ask how happy they are with the relationship on a scale of 1-10** (10 being high). You can also ask them, **"How can I make it a 10?"** This will help give you the information you need to attain the relationship goals you desire.

Using the 1-10 scale strategy can also help communicate issues of importance with your partner such as, "This issue affects me at the level of a 7 or 8." Or you can use the scale to explain how much relief you would get using numbers. An example is: "If you'd be willing to work fewer hours each week, my stress level would decrease by 9 points." This method can help guys, especially, to get an idea of how serious an issue is. Often, spouses get exasperated with the other, when they tell them there is a problem, and things don't change. **Using a number scale to communicate issues, helps to make things more concrete and understandable.** This way partners can more accurately assess the damage and adjust as necessary.

Other Tips for Couples for Connection

For couples who like to compete – *Make a habit of spending time playing a game each day, such as connect four or chess, etc.* Take turns playing each other's favorite game/s. This will help meet your need for competition and keep you from bickering in the bedroom.

Another connection tip follows **for empty nesters who fight about the position of the toilet seat.** Consider making the toilet ready for the other one by women pulling the seat up and men putting the seat down before washing hands. This way it's ready, when each needs to use it (most of the time).

For couples who are renovating a living space - Remodeling a living space can be very hard on a couple, due to things being disorganized and the financial burden and unexpected costs associated with remodeling.

If you are doing the work yourselves and are working together, it's important to **connect by establishing a project leader for the day**. The other person will be their assistant.

If both of you want to do the same thing, take turns. *Also, take turns if* neither one of you wants to do something that needs to be done or ask someone else to do it.

Do together only the things you can agree on together. It eliminates squabbling.

If one of you does not feel safe with the project, STOP immediately and pay attention! Listen to each other! Safety is a must!

There may be times you may want to agree to do things independently - when you don't agree on the method. Or you may want to take turns doing it the other person's way. If neither way works well for one or both of you, *try a third (different) way*.

How to maintain ourselves (who we are), while serving the other?

1. **State how you understand the other person is feeling or what they are needing.**
2. **Tell the other person your feelings and needs** (even if they don't ask)
3. **Assume/Think the best of each other.** (Perception affects behavior)
4. **Tell yourself, and the other person, the truth.** Acknowledge each other's position and efforts.
5. **Think the best of each other.**
6. **Say "No" when needed.**

How to say "No."

First of all, you have permission to say "No."

Secondly, the more you practice saying "No," the easier it gets.

Thirdly, if you can say "No" in a way you feel good about, it's best, so guilt does not set in. Say it with a tone of self-acceptance and without trying to make the other person feel bad for asking.

Fourth, acknowledging the other person's situation, or need, (as well as your own) is half the battle.

Finally, stick with your answer!

We all want understanding love and respect, even when we don't agree or when our needs are conflicting.

Thoughts for Connecting

Communication is the way we connect as humans, be it through words or actions. Next are some final communication examples for connecting with the ones we love.

This is a bit of a review of relationship basics.

1. Imagine yourself in the other person's *shoes*.

"I can understand. I felt like that when ..."

> **a. What might they need?**
>
> *"I can see you're in a tough spot, may I help with something or give you an idea?"*
>
> **b. How might they feel?**
> *"That's a bummer! How frustrating!"*

2. Check it out (examples below)

- *"You look sad. Would you like to talk?"*

- *"You sound angry. Are you mad at me?"*

- *"You look confused. Can I clarify?"*

Other verbal examples to connect at times of stress and nurture the relationship.

"It appears you might be feeling confused. I'm feeling frustrated. Would you be willing to listen to understand what I'm saying?"

"I need time to calm down and get something to eat. Do you mind if we talk after supper about this? That will help me to listen better."

"I like when the house is kept clean. It helps me function better and feel peaceful."

"Would you be willing to put things back where they belong?"

"Would you be willing to help me establish a home for certain items, so we can find them more easily?"

"I like when you help me make dinner. It keeps me company and I feel closer to you."

"You are a good person because..."

"I know you love me when ..."

"I'm sorry I did not do as I promised. What can I do to make it up to you?"

"I realize I was stressed and may have sounded angry with you when I was worried about ..."

"You are important to me. I need you to understand my situation. Although I did not respond the way you would have liked, your happiness is important."

"I understand. When I _____, I felt the same way."

"I'm not sure what that would be like. Can you tell me more?"

"I can see you're in a tough spot, may I help with something or give a suggestion?"

"That's a bummer! How frustrating!"

"You look sad. Would you like to talk?"

"You sound angry. Are you frustrated with me, or is it something else?"

"You look confused. Can I clarify something?"

"How/what can I communicate more clearly?"

As a final note, **I would like to encourage you to be patient with yourself as you work to connect with the person you love and create peace.** *The past is over. That was then. This is now. Be patient with the one you love. Ask them to partner with you to incorporate affirmations and new practices into your relationship. Take notes and practice the new behavior or affirmations you desire over and over until they become more natural and become new habits for you. It gets easier with time.*

Also, **while there may be times when one has to lower their expectations in order to be happy,** *one must not underestimate their power to affect positive changes within a relationship, even if one seemingly has an uncooperative partner at first.* The more you make positive consistent changes, the other person ultimately has no choice, but to respond differently to your new purposeful behavior.

Finally, **be sure to take care of yourself. The better you are, the better you connect.**

Bibliography

Bair, Bonnie (2021) Authentic Peace

Bair, Bonnie (2021) Dealing with Negative Emotions

Bair, Bonnie (2017) Life 101 Affirmations

Bair, Bonnie (2017) We Smile: Communication and Cooperation Strategies for Healing, Intimacy and Teamwork

Burns, David (2002) Conference on Couples Counseling: a Cognitive Behavioral Approach

Chapman, Gary (2004) The Five Love Languages

Eggerichs, Emerson (2004) Love and Respect,

Jordan, Bob (2003) Conference on Bipolar Disorder in Adults, Children and Adolescents using the DSM-IV

Hegstrom, Paul (1990) Class on Learning to Live, Learning to Love

Johnson, Matthew (2001) Positive Parenting with a Plan

Procyk, Anne (2019) 3 Day Conference on Nutrition for Mental Health

Smalley, Gary (1993) Hidden Keys to Loving Relationships

Tracy, Brian (1998) Success Seminar, Peoria, Illionis

Books by Bonnie Bair

Available on Amazon

Authentic Peace (2021)

Bi-polar Disorder in This Up and Down World

COUPLES CONNECT: ENRICH YOUR LOVE LIFE (2024)

FEELINGS and NEEDS (2024) – (for children)

God's Wonder Working Power in Our Lives (2021)

Life 101 Affirmations (2017) – (large print)

Parenting Affirmations (2017) – (large print)

Prayer: Discover the Power Within

Marriage Matters: Marriage Affirmations (2017)

Relationship Maps for Couples Co-workers and College Roommates: Living/Working Peacefully Together

We Smile: Communication and Cooperation Strategies for Healing, Intimacy and Teamwork (2017)

www.ingramcontent.com/pod-product-compliance
Lightning Source LLC
Chambersburg PA
CBHW071220090426
42736CB00014B/2905

Discover relationship secrets and tried and true communication techniques for deepening your relationship and creating peace.

Look inside to find everything from overcoming the past and managing emotions and medical issues, like bipolar disorder, to working as a team in handling finances, children and chores.

The "Relationship Map for Happiness," within, is designed to guide couples in exploring and fulfilling the unrealized needs of each other.

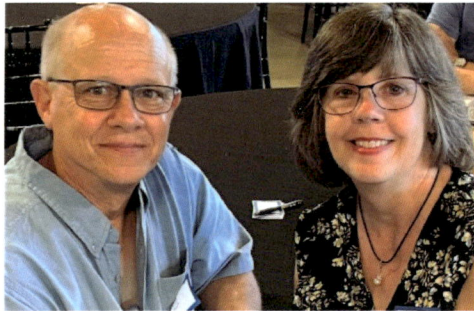

The author's education and expertise are in the areas of communications, human relations, and rehabilitation. She has worked with couples for twelve years and has been married to her husband for over thirty.

STERLING HOUSE PUBLISHING

ISBN 9798985417142

90000

9 798985 417142